HOW TO WRITE FOR THE PROFESSIONAL JOURNALS

Recent Titles from Quorum Books

Res Judicata and Collateral Estoppel: Tools for Plaintiffs and Defendants
Warren Freedman

The Investment Performance of Corporate Pension Plans: Why They Do Not Beat the Market Regularly
Stephen A. Berkowitz, Louis D. Finney, and Dennis E. Logue

Foreign Plaintiffs in Products Liability Actions: The Defense of Forum Non Conveniens
Warren Freedman

A Guide to Hazardous Materials Management: Physical Characteristics, Federal Regulations, and Response Alternatives
Aileen Schumacher

Forecasting Sales with the Personal Computer: Guidelines for Marketing and Sales Managers
Dick Berry

Entrepreneurship and Public Policy: Can Government Stimulate Business Startups?
Benjamin W. Mokry

Handbook of the Money and Capital Markets
Alan Gart

Envisionary Management: A Guide for Human Resources Professionals in Management Training and Development
William P. Anthony, E. Nick Maddox, and Walter Wheatley, Jr.

Marketing Real Estate Internationally
M. A. Hines

Advertising Self-Regulation and Outside Participation: A Multinational Comparison
J. J. Boddewyn

The New Environment in International Accounting: Issues and Practices
Ahmed Belkaoui

Legal Structure of International Textile Trade
Henry R. Zheng

Accounting for Data Processing Costs
Robert W. McGee

The Management of Corporate Business Units: Portfolio Strategies for Turbulent Times
Louis E. V. Nevaer and Steven A. Deck

HOW TO WRITE FOR THE PROFESSIONAL JOURNALS

A Guide for Technically Trained Managers

RYLE L. MILLER, JR.

Quorum Books
New York • Westport, Connecticut • London

Library of Congress Cataloging-in-Publication Data

Miller, Ryle L.
  How to write for the professional journals : a guide for technically trained managers / Ryle L. Miller, Jr.
    p. cm.
  Includes index.
  ISBN 0–89930–254–8 (lib. bdg. : alk. paper)
  1. Technical writing. I. Title.
T11.M49 1988
808'.066—dc 19   87–32592

British Library Cataloguing in Publication Data is available.

Copyright © 1988 by Ryle L. Miller, Jr.

All rights reserved. No portion of this book may be reproduced, by any process or technique, without the express written consent of the publisher.

Library of Congress Catalog Card Number: 87–32592
ISBN: 0–89930–254–8

First published in 1988 by Quorum Books

Greenwood Press, Inc.
88 Post Road West, Westport, Connecticut 06881

Printed in the United States of America

The paper used in this book complies with the Permanent Paper Standard issued by the National Information Standards Organization (Z39.48-1984).

10 9 8 7 6 5 4 3 2 1

This book is dedicated to C. Roland Bridges,
M.D. Without his non-verbal professional
thinking, this book would not have been
completed on schedule.

CONTENTS

	Preface	ix
1.	You and the English Language	1
2.	Prose with a Purpose	17
3.	Words That Share	45
4.	Words with Too Much Meaning	71
5.	An Audience for Your Prose	101
6.	An Offer They Can Not Refuse	127
	Notes	151
	Exercises: Examples for Chapter 3	155
	Exercises: Examples for Chapter 4	165
	Index	175

PREFACE

This work is organized around the assumption that professionally trained people have non-verbalized thoughts worth publishing. It starts with examples of non-verbalized thoughts and proceeds through a succession of problems related to organizing thought for presentation: giving the organized thoughts graceful expression, writing clearly, choosing a medium of publication, getting published, and catching the attention of the reader. Many of these problems have been discussed in books and articles in the fields of psychology, linguistics, and journalism, so that readers who know those fields may expect to find here much that is familiar. I am sincerely sorry to have to disappoint them. Instead of the accepted approaches to writing and journalism, this book presents results of personal experience gained under crisis conditions.

At age thirty-five, at mid-span in a successful career as a design engineer, after a year-long leave spent trying to learn to write, I took a job as a technical reporter for a weekly news magazine, in order to further pursue a writing skill. Although my previous responsibilities for clear writing had gone no further than business letters and project descriptions, the reporter's job required me to produce for publication a news article every week. Otherwise I could expect to be fired. Because I had passed over the currently available jobs in my speciality when taking the reporter's job, and because my salary as a reporter was only a fraction of my previous engineer's salary, success in writing became frighteningly necessary. Fortunately, three things worked in my favor. First, the editors who reviewed my writing were highly skilled and patient. After requiring me to rewrite early articles as many as five times, they would themselves rewrite them again to make them acceptable. Second, my engineering background allowed me to skim over much of the time-consuming research necessary for most technical reporters. Third, the office where I worked was located in midtown Manhattan, where there was ready access to public libraries, writing courses at various universities, book reviews in publications such as *Science*, and reading lists from New York University, where my wife was studying for a master's degree in French literature.

Quite naturally, my first inclination was to turn to popular and academic publications on the elements of style, English usage, journalism, and so forth. Although such publications may be adequate for thinking and talking about writing, they failed to meet the needs of a beginning writer expected to produce clear prose for publication at regular intervals. This failure of conventional texts led to a frantic search for principles that could be applied to writing in the same manner that technical principles can be applied to design calculations. Hundreds of books were collected and studied, so that their concepts rested like tumblers in a lock, waiting for the suitable combinations of problems into which they could fall. This book's brief list of notes shows the sources of the concepts that worked; and the first four chapters impose an order on the haphazard sequence in which those concepts were discovered.

Surprisingly, the concepts that enabled me to write on demand all came out of well-established empirical studies not usually associated with journalism. A conventionalist who wants to dispute the approach taken in this book should defer challenging my sources in favor of challenging my application of those sources, while somehow avoiding the evidence that the application has worked, not once or twice, but hundreds of times.

Otherwise, users of this book may want to keep alert to an underlying bias that can affect the conclusions. More than 95 percent of the publications relied on for experience here have been anonymous. The early articles were nearly all published anonymously, and later articles were anonymously edited for other authors. This anonymous writing certainly has a disorienting effect on my understanding of the motives for writing, particularly when I wrap all those motives up in one expression used to introduce Chapter 5: "The pay is the prestige." My recompense for writing is the satisfaction gained from motivating people to take action and do something. Thus with this book, I hope to motivate you to successfully write and publish significant prose.

It seems pertinent to all this that, for the past nine years, Dolly Miller and I have been living in a house we designed and built with our hands in the midst of a 100-acre woods in the densely forested Northeast Kingdom of Vermont. We have shared experiences; and if the nineteen years of study for this book could be summarized as "thought and language," analogous studies carried out by Dolly Miller over the same period could be called "thought and shaped-colors." However, she does not have the words for such a summary description; she has, instead, her paintings, which are difficult for some people to read.

1

YOU AND THE ENGLISH LANGUAGE

INTRODUCTION TO CHAPTER 1: TOOLS FOR THINKING

During early summer, twenty-one months before I wrote this, I built a sugar house, whose design and construction demonstrate an essential principle of this book on writing. The term *sugar house* is the name given to the buildings used to house evaporators across the northeastern United States and southern Canada, where fresh run maple sap is boiled to syrup in early spring. Generally, sugar houses conform to one of two types imposed by the economics of maple syrup production. Because the sap runs for only about six weeks, and the equipment sits idle for the rest of the year, optimum economics favor inexpensive equipment and relatively high operating costs; and the emphasis on low investment for equipment leads to sugar houses that are either shacks located off in the woods, where they provide minimum shelter for boiling sap collected from nearby trees, or multipurpose buildings, that can serve as restaurants, dance-halls, bars, or salesrooms for the months outside the sugaring season.

My sugar house came under the category of shack. However, it also had complementary and unique purposes. I had invented a novel evaporator system and designed a prototype of that system under contract with a leading manufacturer of conventional evaporators. We proposed to use solutions of granulated sugar to test the prototype during summer and fall, and then to demonstrate it the following spring on maple sap collected from trees on the hillside above the sugar house. Once the demonstration was over, the prototype would have served its purpose, and would be moved to another site. Thus the sugar house was going to be temporary. Also, because it would constitute the environment under which observers watched the tests and demonstrations, and because the prototype represented a conceptually different approach to syrup production, the ideal sugar house would have to be aesthetically pleasing, as well as functional. It was to consist entirely of standardized pieces of lumber held together with screws and lag bolts.

The design chosen to meet these requirements comprised a building 24 feet long and 12 feet wide, with walls 8 feet high, and with four 6-feet high, 2-feet wide windows spaced high along each of the side walls. With a peaked roof, whose sides sloped at 3:1, these proportions gave the building the aspect of a small chapel; they also allowed the use of standardized pieces of lumber, as follows:

The end walls were each made of three standard 4×8 plywood panels, set vertically, with the middle panel on the front end sawed down the middle and hinged on its sides to make a double door. The side walls were composed of two vertical, standard 4×8 panels, plus the four windows, plus four 2×8 panels sawed from two standard 4×8 panels, for spacers beside the windows. One additional 4×8 panel was sawed into eight $2' \times 2'$ panels to fit under the windows. Each sloping side of the roof was 28 feet by 8 feet, so that it could be composed of seven standard 4×8 panels.

Supports for this shell were standard $2'' \times 8''$ planks 8 feet long. These pieces were located standing on one end at 2-foot intervals along the walls and ends, and were fabricated into roof trusses, which were also placed at 2-foot intervals. Each truss consisted of the standard $2'' \times 8''$ planks joined at the peak end by a metal plate and held at the required angle by a $1'' \times 6''$ board 12 feet long, which spanned from one side wall to the other. These $1'' \times 6''$ truss boards rested on a "plate" composed of the standard $1'' \times 6''$ boards fastened across the top ends of the wall-support planks and overlapping the edges of other $1'' \times 6''$ boards fastened along the top outside edges of those planks. This caused the 4×8 panels to extend 6 inches below the bottoms of the wall-support planks, so that the panels could be fastened to the outside edge of a 6-inch-high footing built up of three layers of the standard planks bolted together.

Now, the preceding six paragraphs are the first written documentation ever applied to that sugar house. Except for some numbers jotted down to keep count of the standard pieces to be purchased, the entire design was worked out mentally. There were no sketches or words. In effect, this sugar house, which required thought and decisions, was articulated into physical reality entirely without the benefit of words. That non-verbal articulation, which still stands, demonstrates conclusively a principle that serves as the first step into this book: Thought, particularly the thought of professional people, exists independently of language; writing for professional publication almost always requires that the writer attach words to independent thoughts that already exist but have never before been verbalized; and that problem of verbalization is the first problem to be understood by professional people who would write.

It is often said that the statement of a problem is 90 percent of its solution. That, unfortunately, does not hold for the problem of attaching words to non-verbal thinking, because users of the English language have emphasized verbal thought so much that we have relatively little understanding of thinking that is not advanced through words. Furthermore, professional thinking varies from one profession to the other; medical doctors, lawyers, accountants, biologists, engineers, chemists, physicists, mathematicians, and so on, all think differently—so differently that the conventional practice is to ignore the effects that professional thought does have on language.

Consequently, a first step toward writing for professional publications should be a subjective inward look at one's private thought processes. This takes effort. Although you do think all the time, you also walk, feel, see, hear, taste, and use your hands and arms; and it is a safe bet that you do not know how you do those things. Yet walking can be seen and analyzed, whereas no one sees your thinking. On the other hand, exactly because you are a professional, you have acquired formal tools for thinking within your profession. These can be identified, and once you have done that, you can squeeze through the eye of this needle into a world where you confront and direct your own thought processes. You are in the position of a talented amateur athlete, who does not know how he or she performs—only that the performance does take place. You now try to become aware of what you are already doing well, in order that you will be able to do it better—consciously. For a while, as one after another of your customary actions is shifted from intuitive to conscious control, your game will suffer. But in the end your performance will improve—not by degrees, but categorically. It has been demonstrated many times over.

Its relative simplicity suggests the above description of the sugar house as a demonstration for the manner in which parts of a formal discipline can be used directly for thinking. In the case of the sugar house, the discipline is "farm carpentry"; and the parts of this discipline are the familiar dimensions of standard plywood panels and lumber pieces. With those dimensions functioning as part of one's mental vocabulary, it takes only a moment's half-conscious reflection to choose overall dimensions that are multiples of the plywood panels: 24' × 12' chosen before 28, 20, 16, or 8. And so forth. From this basis, it is equally easy to determine the rest of the construction in terms of equivalencies of those dimensions.

From this, it is possible to proceed by analogy to identify thinking tools for other disciplines. In this analogy, one should search to identify, first, the equivalents of the sugar house's dimensions, and then, the equivalents of the standard dimensions of the pieces of lumber. Because all of the equivalents are integral parts of one's thinking, the projected items may seem overly simple. However, their simplicity will be in direct proportion to their power. This can be demonstrated by an application within chemical engineering.

Although chemical engineers are supposed to be cognizant of such wide-ranging fields as metallurgy, thermodynamics, organic chemistry, thermochemistry, physics, and catalysis, the primary function of a design chemical engineer can be described simply as moving materials into and out of chemical reactions and associated separation processes. Consequently, the essential parts of any chemical engineering design (corresponding to the sugar house dimensions) are material balances and heat balances; and the units for thinking in terms of heat and material balances (corresponding to the standard pieces of lumber) are units of mass, heat, and the mass equivalent of the molecular weight. That is all.

Although this may seem to be an oversimplification, analyses show that heat and material balances are the bases for the gamut of chemical engineering calculations, from distillation to reaction kinetics to furnace design. Ingenious methods for balancing heat into and out of operations have been the bases for powerful graphs and economic analyses,[1] as well as for improvements in complex processes.[2] However, it is obviously beyond the scope of this book to project tools of professional thought for fields beyond the author's experience. The reader is urged to make such projections based on a combination of training and personal experience. From that basis, recognizing that each of us comes to the common ground of clear English prose with individual tools for thinking, this book will present a circuit of concepts that transcend individual differences.

The last half of the twentieth century has seen the emergence of various scientific and technical observations that can lead to new viable concepts when used to solve long-standing problems of clear writing. These observations come to us from such wide-ranging disciplines as computer science, developmental psychology, scientific linguistics, communications engineering, and statistical analysis. All pragmatic and empirical, they are for the most part thirty years old, or older, at the time of this writing. Consequently, they have been sometimes overlooked or forgotten, because they have come before the times of the problems they solve. Taken together, however, they do work to provide a clear and consistent method for bringing the most complex thoughts into clear verbal expression. We begin by comparing scientific and technical thinking with logic.

VERBAL TOOLS: LOGIC AND CONCEPTS

"The ancient Greeks, in working out their principles for prose, found that they could not confine themselves to Orthology (a study of the proper formation of words), Accidence (a study of the grammatical relation of words) and Syntax (a study of the grammatical relation of phrases and sentences); they had to include Logic, which is the study of the proper relation of ideas."[3] Ever since the Greeks formulated their principles of logic, astronomers, chemists, physicists, and others have continued to relate ideas, often producing unexpected results for which the relationships are more important than the ideas proper.

In the field of chemistry, for example. A. L. Lavoisier and P. S. Laplace (1780) determined that the quantity of heat needed to decompose chemical compounds equals the heat released when those same compounds are formed out of the decomposition elements. Subsequently, G. H. Hess (1840) determined that this "heat of formation" is the same whether the composition or decomposition takes place in one or several stages. Still later, G. R. Kirchoff (1855) determined that the heat of formation changes with temperature, and he worked out a formula for the amount of the change. A few years later (1864), C. M. Guldberg and P. Wage determined that the rate at which chemical compounds are formed is proportional to the reactive masses of the substances and measurable in terms of a corresponding "equilibrium constant."

To this, Henry L. Chatelier (1850–1936) added the observation that a change in the conditions of a chemical system in equilibrium caused that system to react to accommodate the change; and Le Chatelier's principle thus introduced the effects of temperature and pressure on equilibrium constants. Almost concurrently, J. H. Van't Hoff (1896) determined an exact expression for the equilibrium constant in terms of temperature and the heat of formation at constant pressure. This led to the determination of "standard free energies," which can be added and subtracted to determine the heat of formations for many different compounds; and by applying the appropriate formulae, it is possible to estimate the effects of temperature and pressure on the heat of formation and to determine conditions of equilibrium in, for example, a fire.

Similarly related groups of ideas are found in engineering where, for example, the notion of equivalence between "stress" on a beam and its corresponding elastic distortion or "strain" has led to the idea of a "modulus of elasticity" that has been determined and recorded for most construction materials. When those materials are used in designated shapes, the modulus of elasticity and the allowable strain are related to specific conditions through the "moment of inertia" specific to those shapes.

In contrast to the logic of the ancient Greeks, these relations of ideas do not concern themselves with "truth" or "good" or "evil"; instead they attempt to project knowledge from known situations into the unknown, often along a curve that can be plotted on graph paper. Also, scientific and technical principles do not depend on the conventional devices of reasoning; instead they depend on concepts, such as the concepts of chemical heat of formation, equilibrium constant, and standard free energy, or the engineering concepts of stress-strain, modulus of elasticity, and moment of inertia.

Such conceptual thinking has separated the reasoning of science and technology from the ancient dependence on prose. Whereas logicians have asserted that truth must be liable to expression in words, scientific and technical people are satisfied with a mathematical formula, the concentration of a solution, or a chart. Although scientists do think with language, "the most important fact uncovered through the genetic study of thought and speech is that their relationship undergoes many changes. Progress in thought and progress in speech are not parallel. Their growth curves cross and recross. They may straighten out and run side by side, even merge for a time, but they always diverge again."[4] Thus many modern people pursue entire careers during which their progress in thinking is separated from their language. This is unfortunate, because it alienates such people from other speakers of their native language, and fails to exploit the real tool for thought that is available in language. This book attempts to overcome such problems through an approach to language that is pragmatic and technical rather than poetic or artistic; its principles are based on concepts, which are in turn based on empirical tests.

VERBAL TOOLS: CLASSES OF THOUGHT

The focal point of the principles to be presented in this book is a collection of about 500 articles, written or edited by the author over the course of seventeen years, and published in the journals *Chemical Week* and *Chemical Engineering*, where those articles were exposed to more than sixty thousand readers, and measured for effect through reader surveys. The writing in each of those articles was conceived as an experiment made according to the principle of substitution. Technical examples of this principle are the substitution of different coupons of metal in a standard corrosion test rack, or the substitution of different organic compounds in a standard reagent, or the application of different reagents to a given compound.

In the case of the articles, a standard article outline was used; and thoughts were substituted into the different parts of that outline. There were six parts to the outline, and if a thought could fit one of those six parts it was classified accordingly. The first several hundred of the articles were published in *Chemical Week* during 1960–1966. These were news articles, and they were obliged to conform to the magazine's style and format. In general, they began by describing some current activity or condition, often accompanied by the expression "this week." Because the U.S. chemical industry during those years was at a high point of competitive activity, the activity or condition was introduced in such a way as to suggest that here was a company or group of people who were winning a competitive edge over the reader.

In order to make this suggestion more forceful, the second part of the article stated that the activity or condition solved a problem, which was described in terms that would make it appreciated by the widest possible number of readers. Next, in a manner to hold the reader's attention, a technical explanation was offered to show how and why the activity or condition offered a solution of the problem. This explanation was offered in succinct generalities so as to be easily understood and suggest that the technical solution was something that the reader ought to have thought of for his or her self. Then in order to convince the reader that the actors in the article were indeed gaining a competitive advantage (and that the reader should consequently do something about it), the article next offered background information and data to make the succinct explanation more convincing. This was accompanied by a description of sources of such information. Finally, to protect the magazine's authoritative position, the article offered some possible weaknesses in the technical reasoning of the explanation.

These were serious, commercially effective articles, which could in no way be restricted by their parallel purpose of experimenting with the classification of thought. Some articles had major effects on multimillion dollar contracts, others promulgated widespread use of new technology, and others noticeably affected relationships within the chemical industry.

Now, it takes about seven years for a new chemical manufacturing process to be carried from laboratory studies to fruition in a manufacturing plant. What stage of that seven-year development should be selected for "this week" treatment in *Chemical Week*? Most chemical manufacturing processes are sequences of unit operations that must all function cooperatively like links in a chain. Which unit operation should be selected to represent the solution to the problem solved by a given process? Since every aspect of modern chemical technology depends on a vast body of concepts and data that could never be summarized in a short news article, what parts of that vast body should be chosen for presentation in a given article?

Surprisingly, all those questions could be answered by one word: *expediency*. Typically, writing an article required only about 20 percent of the total time required for its preparation; about 50 percent of the time was consumed by interviews, literature searches, and calculations; and some 30 percent was taken up in persuading managing editors of the article's importance, checking galley proofs, reviewing illustrations, and so forth. With little time available for writing, there was none available for nuances of expression or searching out apt words. The available thoughts were mentally scanned for their suitability to fit one or more of the positions, and then put there. If the article involved a manufacturing process, for example, that unit operation requiring the most explanation (and thus longer, more elaborate article) was selected as the solution to the problem and frequently introduced as "the key." The "this week" introduction could be the issuance of a patent, activity at a construction site, a contract, or a paper given at a technical meeting. And the problem was invented to suit. The magazine had a policy of never complicating a single article with more than one central idea, so there were no opportunities to compound the simple outline.

As the growing number of successfully published articles afforded increasing confidence and familiarity with the various positions in the standard outline, an ever wider variety of thoughts were tried in each position. Although the magazine's management imagined, for example, that the connotation of news was essential to the introduction, ever more varied substitutions revealed that the underlying principle behind the so-called news is a connotation of reality. This led to the successful use of a chart or photograph for the introduction. The article would typically begin with, "The photo above shows..." (some activity at a construction site, a newly constructed plant, etc.).

After some two hundred such articles had been published, I left *Chemical Week* and went to *Chemical Engineering* to edit articles by others, which presented the classification of thoughts from a different point of view. No matter how successful the *Chemical Week* experiments had been, there always was a suspicion that they had been molded to fit the theory, and that the classification of thought represented more ingenuity than fact. The edited articles, by contrast, came from literally all over the world, from many authors whose native language was not English.

Enthusiastically plunging into the new job, I would start by skimming a new article to identify the six parts (which at this time were *Classes I* through *VI*). In view of my past experience, the work should have been easy; but almost immediately, I found myself unable to mentally take hold of the articles in the way necessary to rearrange them. Perhaps I had been deluding myself. Perhaps the intelligence and technical background required for these articles were beyond me. I was reduced to muddling through the articles line by line and paragraph by paragraph, the normal way for most editors. The overall mood was often that of failing to completely grasp the subject and of incompetence. The sensation was that of a person trying to play a game of cards without sorting the cards that have been dealt, and gaping in confusion while everyone else moves on briskly with the game.

Just as the crisis was reaching a climax, there came to mind an old-fashioned cure for the hiccups: Think all at once of four horses struggling individually to pull a heavy wagon. The required concentration is supposed to calm the nervous spasms of the hiccups and make them go away. But why should there be no more and no less than four horses? Perhaps six categories of thought were too many. By way of experiment, classes IV, V, and VI were grouped arbitrarily into one class (IV) for the next article; and the editing of that article seemed almost to go by itself. The conclusion is that, in organizing information, one should not create more than four categories. Note that there are four playing-card suits (clubs, hearts, diamonds, and spades), four cardinal points on the compass, four seasons in the year, four word classes (nouns, verbs, adjectives, and adverbs), and an endless list of other examples. The rule of four thus suggests one way in which language effectively impinges on thought through formal constraints that match but do not exceed the limits of human intelligence.[5]

With an arbitrary classification of four classes of thought, editing technical articles became easy. And since reader surveys were conducted on all issues of *Chemical Engineering*, it was possible to measure the effect of every editing effort. Within a short period of time, confirmation from reader surveys had removed all doubts. Other editors and writers were canvassed for words that might aptly describe the four parts of the frame article; and the four class numbers were replaced by the terms *situation, problem, resolution,* and *information,* so that the classification was called the SPRI system.

My practice was to skim a new manuscript to see what the author wanted to say and to designate that thought as R in the margin of the manuscript. Next, those thoughts suggesting a problem resolved by the R thought were identified with a P in the margin. Then those thoughts that either led to the problem or provided background for the resolution were identified with S or I, respectively. When all the thoughts had been classified in this manner, the order of thoughts in each class was indicated with subscript numbers. Surprisingly, it was not necessary to create bridge phrases to string together thoughts assembled from remote parts of a given manuscript; and many bridge phrases that the original authors had felt necessary could be removed. The time required for SPRI editing was only about half normal; and the quality of the editing suggested a thorough command of the technology.

The edited versions of the articles were always sent to the authors, along with a brief description of SPRI, for prepublication review. Although the SPRI editing drastically changed most articles, its acceptance by authors was remarkably good. Because they could find and identify all their original thoughts, many authors saw the editing as no more than, say, a change of scale on a chart. Given some three hundred articles, less than a dozen authors objected. These, remembered because of their scarcity, show interesting similarities. Two objections came from magazine writers, three from Orientals for whom English was a second language, and two from young authors who had never been published before. All these people felt that the editor's prerogatives had been overextended in changing their personal style.

However, attempts to discuss the findings of SPRI experiments met with resistance from professional editors and writers. Such people had already established their own work habits, and regarded prose composition as a skill that can not be learned in the manner of mathematics and chemistry. Yet it was other writers who forced the SPRI experiments into their next stage of development. For such writers, a classification was not enough; they demanded rules. The demands became a challenge; and once started, the search for rules relating SPRI led beyond language into psychology and communications engineering.

MENTAL TOOLS: LEVELS OF THOUGHT, CONCEPTS, UNCERTAINTY

Involved are levels of thought, uncertainty, and the nature of concepts, all working together. In order for the reader to conceptualize these ideas, you should study the two columns of words below. Left to right, identical words are used, but in a different order. In each instance, the signal word, *the*, precedes two words normally classed as nouns; but the sequence of those two words is reversed, left to right, with a consequent change of meaning. You should try to describe that change in meaning, making a sincere, imaginative effort, even though you know in advance that a studied description is going to be offered later on. Make notes on a piece of paper. Do not assume that, just because it has been discussed in books on syntax, you already understand this phenomenon; there is more than syntax involved. As you make your effort, realize that you are attempting to articulate two discrete levels of thought while performing your own private experiment in concept formation and psychological uncertainty. Here are the words:

the house dog	the dog house
the pocket watch	the watch pocket
the glass eye	the eye glass
the ring finger	the finger ring
the horse cart	the cart horse
the catalyst base	the base catalyst
the phase equilibrium	the equilibrium phase
the signal word	the word signal

If you compare the meanings of a given noun as it is shifted from the middle to the final position, you will see that it tends to assume its dictionary meaning in the final position, where its meaning is stable yet flexible enough to cover different types of the same object; it is discrete, articulated, and definite. By contrast, the words in the middle position are labile, in that their meaning takes on the meaning of the following word, but rigid in that their meaning is broken by a change in the following word; they are syncretic, diffuse, and indefinite.

These groups of properties—stable, flexible, discrete, articulated, and definite, versus labile, rigid, syncretic, diffuse, and indefinite—are discussed by Heinz Werner, where they are used to characterize *cognitive* versus *primitive* thinking.[6] In chapters devoted to pairs of opposed properties (stable/labile, flexible/rigid, etc.), Werner shows that primitive thinking, with its identified properties, dominates children, psychopaths, and primitive people, whereas cognitive thinking is achieved only by mature people capable of forming concepts.

Similar findings have been reported by Jean Piaget, who describes the change from primitive to cognitive as "decentralization" to indicate the change from subjective to objective thinking that is involved. Other extensions of the concept have been applied to psychological testing for the ability to cope with modern life.[7] Also, various reports by anthropologists show how initiation ceremonies of primitive peoples often serve to arrest the development of cognitive thinking, which tends generally to make its appearance at puberty. It would appear that the objectivity of cognitive thinking might otherwise disrupt the tightly knit social structures of those societies.

While none of the above mentioned studies attempted to relate the level of thought to syntax, it can be seen immediately from the two columns of word groups that the meanings of the sixteen nouns exist either in the primitive mode or the cognitive mode depending on their positions in the sixteen word groups. Furthermore, experiments with thoughts in SPRI, as well as phrases in published sentences, show that the same primitive/cognitive relation holds true for all parts of prose. Consequently, language has been shown to act as a complex of syntactic signals that put words, phrases, and entire thoughts into either the primitive or cognitive mode, similar to the manner in which digital computers use either/or responses to articulate alternative parts of a program.

Returning to the sixteen word groups and the reader's private experiment in concept formation, it is time to ask if the reader holds concepts of *primitive* and *cognitive* as distinct modes of thought, and to describe how those concepts may have been derived. Note that there has been no attempt to present the concepts of primitive and cognitive thought as consequences of theories, reasoning, or forms of logic. Instead, a phenomenon was presented, and the reader was asked to address the problem of describing that phenomenon; then there was offered a widely accepted characterization of that phenomenon, along with two symbols for that characterization, the words *primitive* and *cognitive*. Finally, the reader was asked to believe that this symbolized characterization is stable within language and applies outside the eighteen three-word examples. The key step in this process was the reader's voluntarily attempting to describe in advance the two modes of thought. Success in forming a new concept depends on a willingness to enter into uncertainty; and *uncertainty*, coming after levels of *thought* and *concepts*, is the last of our triumvirate of concepts. Uncertainty has been conceptualized through the two groups of tests described below.

The first group of tests began in the years following World War I, when veterans with brain damage were treated in Holland by a dedicated doctor who devoted interested sympathy to his patients' problems. This doctor was in the habit of interviewing patients across a table at which they would sit before a square mat on which were placed a writing pad and pencil for making notes. The doctor noticed that, as the interviews were terminated, the patients would always square the writing pad on the mat and put the pencil precisely along the pad. When, out of curiosity, he reached across to put the pencil askew, the patient would rearrange it parallel to the edge of the pad; and if the pencil were again put askew, the patient would again put it right. This little game would continue for as long as the doctor wanted to play it.

If he told the patient to leave the pencil in its askew position, the patient would do so, but with apparent distress.

This pencil-placing game has served as a symbol for a wide range of studies and observations that the doctor, Kurt Goldstein, reports in a book titled *The Organism*.[8] He maintains that the primary human motivation is not sex, aggression, hunting, or other simplistic drives theorized by psychologists, but a complex purpose described as "realizing one's nature." The human is born into a completely unfamiliar, dimly-sensed world. Bit by tiny bit the human infant probes this unknown world, advancing where encouraged and retreating from rebuffs. Each bit of encouragement and rebuff adds to a growing knowledge, which enables the developing infant to probe further afield. "Realizing one's nature" is seen as a desire to increase this knowledge so as to be able to operate more freely and willfully within an ever less-restricted environment.

However, attempts toward realizing one's nature can also lead to anxiety. Different from fear, anxiety is the intimate experience of the unknown, such as can happen on awakening from a dream in a pitch dark room. Anxiety leads to shock, which can be fatal. Thus a constant exploration of one's potential in an unknown environment carries possibilities for reward, in the form of exhilaration from success, or punishment in the form of anxiety. People who have been disabled try to avoid some of these possibilities by surrounding themselves with an ordered environment in which everything is well known. Thus Goldstein's pencil-placing game has been described as "orderliness behavior."

Many studies show that language offers a discrete environment within which a person can adventure to realize his or her nature. But language is safer than real life; no one is known to have died from the shock of a confused sentence or paragraph; yet the symptoms of adventure, anxiety, and orderliness behavior are all there. In fact, all syntax can be regarded as conditioned orderliness behavior, in that we act to accommodate to lessons from past experience. Thus in the above eighteen word groups, the signal word, *the*, caused us to retreat from a subconscious search for meaning until a safe symbol presented itself; and the meanings of the intervening words were derived from that symbol. If the symbol is too long in coming or is confused, it is "bad grammar." Here are some sentences that have correct syntax but which the reader may call bad grammar:

He's the girl I'm going with's brother.

She's the man who tends our garden's mother.

They are the boy who lives here's books.

It's the couple next door's car.

Reading over the above sentences, we see that the last word in each sentence carries a sort of emphasis, because it brought a return to order from relatively extended bouts of linguistic confusion. We might wonder if there were some way of measuring the amount of confusion resolved by those final words. Some measurements have been made. In 1948, a communications engineer at Bell Laboratories, C. E. Shannon, published in the *Bell Systems Technical Journal* an article called "The Mathematical Theory of Communication," in which he reported results of presenting writings to people, letter by letter, and asking them to guess the next letter before it was revealed. The number of required guesses revealed the amount of uncertainty resolved by that letter. And because each guess was answered by a "yes" or "no," this method of measurement is well suited to digital computers; the number of guesses expresses the amount of uncertainty in the "bits" of information used by computer engineers and statisticians. This system has become known as "information theory."

More importantly, Shannon's experiments have shown that information is the opposite equal to uncertainty, so that information theory serves as an extension of Goldstein's realizing our nature. A concentrated form of information consists of knowledge based on concepts, which are the result of successfully resolving an intense form of uncertainty, called "problems." By articulating problems that are then resolved with word symbols, language can serve to promulgate concepts. And because concepts are the stones of which the forms of science and technology are built, this promulgation of concepts is an essential feature of writing for professional publications.

Such writers are always faced with the problem of where within a body of prose the featured concepts should be presented, and then of how the individual sentences and paragraphs should be arranged to give those concepts proper attention. A common but unskillful method consists of supplying numerous headings in bold type, sometimes as many as one for each of several succeeding paragraphs; and within those paragraphs important words are underlined or italicized. Carried to its extreme, such writing is merely the equivalent of an extended table; and one form of experiment with *Chemical Week* articles consisted of reversing that tendency and converting recently developed information from tabular form to columns of prose in news articles.

Another method for organizing prose in suggested by a system of mathematical formulae. Information = uncertainty is extended through the concept of bits of information to statistical analysis, in which the mathematical relations identify two basic forms of uncertainty: conditional uncertainty, and contingent uncertainty. Conditional uncertainty represents the amount of uncertainty information that depends uniquely on the variable in question; contingent uncertainty represents the amount of uncertainty information that depends on associated variables.[9] If we relate conditional uncertainty to the concept *cognitive* and contingent uncertainty to the concept *primitive*, we see that, in the expressions *the eye glass*, *the phase equilibrium*, and *the signal word*, the words *eye*, *phase*, and *signal* represent contingent information, while *glass*, *equilibrium*, and *word* are conditional. We see that the characteristics of the primitive mode (labile, rigid, syncretic, diffuse, indefinite) induce borrowing information from the associated words, whereas the characteristics of the cognitive mode (stable, flexible, articulated, discrete, definite) induce independence. Thus the mathematics of variance in statistics has been identified as a means for measuring the extent to which words or phrases are primitive or cognitive. Also, the mathematical structures can serve as models for constraints external to syntax, as laws of physics are external to the language used to describe them.

And that closes the circuit of concepts that defines this book's approach to writing: Contemporary thinking on a professional level is conceptual. Thoughts have been classified through substitutions in a given prose frame; and this has suggested constraints on thought that are imposed by human mentality. The relations existing between identified classes of thoughts and words have revealed that thinking occurs in either the primitive mode or cognitive mode, the later mode being epitomized by concepts, which can only be formed as a consequence of a problem. Problems in turn relate to uncertainty, which is revealed as the linguistic device that triggers the primitive mode in language, and which has been shown to be measurable and the opposite of information. When the measurements of uncertainty = information are put into a suitable mathematics, those mathematics model the relations between primitive and cognitive modes, as well as between pure thought and pure language. Underlying all is a primary human motive to realize our nature through adventurous exploration, which can be carried out through writing.

HABITS AS TOOLS

With these concepts well in mind, you have all the mental tools you need to write according to the teachings of this book. However, it is unlikely that you have gained the necessary familiarity with these tools. Writing, like almost any other human activity, requires much thinking in the primitive mode. One of the primary advantages of the primitive mode is its speed. At this point, the circuit of concepts is only known consciously, so that their application would necessarily be conscious. Although theoretically feasible this process would be so slow as to be realistically impossible.

Starting now, therefore, the reader should change his or her role, from that of a passive receptacle for thoughts and concepts, to that of an active participant. Rather than accept these thoughts in the verbal packages I give them, you should constantly question. Review this first chapter, its organization and its language. Make notes of your own independent observations. Then recompose and rewrite parts or all of this chapter to suit yourself. This will afford you invaluable experience; you will not only decide what you can believe, but also what you already know intuitively; and you will be constructing a pattern of habits that will become more and more useful as we progress.

Please bear in mind, as you do this, that only one of the many concepts presented here is original. That is the notion of the SPRI classification of thought. Every other concept has been developed by renowned authorities in its field, and has been widely accepted. Any novel applications used in this book are in plain English, for you to evaluate for yourself. Later, in Chapters 3 and 4, there will be some exercises for you to perform in order to strengthen some habits. However, those exercises and those habits will be in the nature of a shell for the structure of habits you will be forming as we go along.

It now remains for me to clothe the concepts from the circuit in the sort of rules and principles that would-be writers like to see. This will take place in three broad categories of composition: First, a review of the thought organizations shown most effective in prose; second, demonstrated methods for holding a reader's interest; and third, a brief glance at some of the facets of scientific linguistics to discover those aspects you most likely will need to make conscious. Specifically, I propose to present explicit instructions on how to become a virtuoso of prose composition (Chapter 2), assemble thoughts for easy and interesting reading (Chapter 3), and choose and arrange words to match the thought (Chapter 4).

After Chapter 4, the subject shifts from the problems of writing to the problems of getting published. From looking inward to thought and its expression, we shall turn outward toward the publishing industry and those of its members who have direct influence on professional publications.

2

PROSE WITH A PURPOSE

INTRODUCTION TO CHAPTER 2: THINKING BY DESIGN

This chapter obeys the promise, made in Chapter 1, "to present explicit instructions on how to...become a virtuoso of prose composition." Unfortunately, that promise can not be fulfilled as readily as it was made, because we must first define what it is that we wish to compose, and that was only suggested in Chapter 1 as "professional publication." Anyone who has enough experience with the thoughts of a profession to want to put them into words knows that such thoughts are difficult to come by. Yet a discussion of prose composition that does not directly involve the objects of that composition—the thoughts—must remain incomplete. This chapter must therefore begin with a look at the thinking of a trained professional before relating that thought to prose.

Fortunately, there is a large source of experience and empirical evidence that, although mostly untapped, does provide what we need to know about the make-up of thinking on a professional level. This source is design—the design of factories, houses, tools, bridges, roads, buildings, dams, machinery, automobiles, furniture—in fact, all man-made objects in the civilized world. Although much that we see has been copied, even those copies come from an original design somewhere—a design through which purposeful thinking turned formless matter into physical objects. Because we tend to avoid uncertainty, we take the existence of designed objects for granted and rarely see the problems involved. Philosophers and psychologists have largely ignored design thinking. Even teachers of science and technology rarely teach professional design, and often behave like the lay community in failing to recognize that a design exists. Yet the objects around us always give testimony to design and design thinking.

Take, for example, the design of a book. We recognize, easily, that a designer has specified the type, page size, layouts, and so on, for purposes of aesthetics and convenience. But what about the paper? It did not just happen. Nor did the factory that made the paper. Nor the cover. Nor the binding. Each of these required thoughtful manufacture by means of machines and equipment that in turn required thoughtful manufacture. And behind all that lies purposeful design thinking in terms of chemistry, mechanics, and so on. Just for a book.

It is by design that the thought classes of *situation*, *problem*, *resolution*, and *information* are parts of prose thinking; they are also parts of design thought. Those names for the four classes of prose thought were actually borrowed from real experience with design activity, and then tested for their recognition with working editors.

In this chapter, we shall first look at design thinking to find the SPRI classes of thought, and to see how SPRI is used in design. Then we shall turn to the use of technical concepts in design, then to the role of problems with their resolutions in creating significance in real life as well as in prose, then to similarities between technical writing and design, then to a review as in design and writing, and finally to explicit instructions for article composition.

THOUGHT PATTERNS APPLIED IN DESIGN

Shortly after World War II, French geologists discovered oil in the southwest of France, in a region called Parentis, not far from the port city of Bordeaux. An American oil company decided to build near Bordeaux a refinery that would process Parentis crude oil, as well as crude oils from Libya, Saudi Arabia, Texas, and Venezuela.

Many plans and commitments were made as part of this refinery project. Ocean-going tankers were dedicated for making shipments from the five different sources of crude oil. Docking facilities were prepared for those tankers at Bordeaux. Storage tanks and piping were designed and built for receiving oil from the tankers and then sending it to the refinery. And additional storage facilities, pipeline systems, and shipping connections were built and dedicated for distributing the products (mostly heating oil, jet fuel, and gasoline) throughout Europe. All of these activities had to be coordinated through the refinery, specifically through the refinery's design, which needed to take account of nine different conditions, in order to be able to accommodate mixtures of the five different crude oils as well as each of the five taken separately.

Although thousands of people were involved in this project, design of the major portions of the refinery was consigned to a single U.S. engineering company with an office in Paris; and final, direct responsibility fell to two U.S. engineers in their early thirties, aided by a crew of seven French engineers still in their twenties.

This design work required unquestionably accurate and clear communication. The dimensions and the specifications of the refinery equipment and its arrangements required detailed, accurate calculations, with units of measure to suit both the French manufacturers and the American sources of the technology. Specific calculations had to be set down and described so that a third party, whether French or American, would be able to review them. And the results of the calculations, which were expressed in myriad sheets of specifications, had to be suitable for use with an accuracy beyond any shadow of doubt. Although the refinery was eventually to exist as steel and concrete, the refinery's design—the calculations, the specifications, the dimensions, everything—existed only as words, numbers, and lines on paper.

Obviously, this design on paper had to translate thinking into the steel and concrete of the refinery. Obviously, this design on paper had to be recognizable and understandable to any of the thousands working to complete the refinery. Consequently, this paper design obviously had to follow a form so reasonable as to be recognized immediately by both French and Americans who worked on the refinery and might be seeing the design for the first time. Furthermore, because this design was fundamentally the same as other designs carried on around the world from before World War II until now, that form of the design continues to find expression everywhere that purposeful thought converts formless matter into useful objects. Without at least a recognition of that form, modern people are forced to stand uncomprehendingly to the side, while designers continue to shape the real world.

What is it, then, that characterizes the form of design thinking?

Since I was one of those young Americans working on the Bordeaux refinery, you might like to know exactly how we went about thinking through that refinery's design, day by day. We advanced the designs in stages. At the beginning of each stage, we would hold an informal meeting at which the previous stage was reviewed and put in the context of the overall purpose. Then the next impending problem was carefully identified and discussed. Thinking together, we would consider how best to solve this problem, relying primarily on our knowledge of the fundamentals. This would lead to a calculation procedure, which was reviewed against other procedures found in the literature or remembered from past experience, then condensed to a minimum number of steps, and (this was before computers) put onto calculation forms. Then we would divide up the forms so that we could all work at once on different parts of the calculation and combine our parts for faster results. Those who finished their parts first were free to start thinking about the next stage of the design. The final result of all this was a "Process Design Manual" consisting of pages in a loose-leaf book about three inches think.

In working together this way, we resembled teams of design engineers working together in engineering companies around the world. Most large projects, such as dams, buildings, bridges, pipelines, and factories, are handled by engineering companies, within which actual design procedures are passed on by word of mouth and proprietary manuals. As individuals acquire experience with those procedures, they come into possession of "know-how," which is described as intellectual property that can be transferred only in the form of a service. Their design know-how thus becomes the property of the individuals. Although there is a tendency for each design organization or company to have procedures that are more or less distinct, the universality of design know-how, as well as the need for engineering companies to work together on large projects, requires that procedures match. They can all be reduced to six criteria essential for any design:

- A basis
- Assumptions
- Specific conditions
- A problem
- A procedure
- Results

The basis for design is a comprehensive statement of the purpose and conditions for the general design. It usually appears in an engineering contract, where it will typically refer to one or more appendices, consisting of drawings, tables, and texts, which define the subject of the design. Without this basis and the appendices, the stated purpose of the design would be too vague to make up the subject of a contract.

The assumptions generally limit a designer's responsibility to accurate thinking. They concern acceptable data, sources of data, and calculation procedures involving correlations. Although assumptions are typically written into a design contract, the first reviews of a project by the design engineers will often bring a flurry of correspondence for purposes of establishing, as assumptions, additional acceptable calculation procedures and data. Because assumptions enter into the nature of design technology, writing assumptions usually requires the purchaser of design work to have professionals as representatives.

Specific conditions grow out of the basis and assumptions, plus that part of the design already accomplished. In the design of a house, for example, the question "For whom?" establishes the basis, while associated assumptions will involve bathroom, sleeping, and dining requirements, and thus the overall plan for the house. When that house is located on a specific site, the conditions of that site—soil, wind, rain, snow, and so on—must be brought in to proceed with designs of foundations and so on.

The design problem is a statement of the requirements imposed by the specific conditions, as for example, how much structure is necessary to resist the prevalent winds blowing against the house. It sometimes takes a sophisticated designer to recognize all the problems imposed by a set of conditions; and most designs that fail do so because of a problem that was overlooked.

The procedure spells out the method for carrying out calculations necessary for solving the design problem. Such procedures are usually taught in universities as "design methods," and various procedures are anticipated in the assumptions. However, the application of a procedure can not be regarded as the resolution of a design problem, as is illustrated in the design for the supports for the roof of a house. Assume a known load and the use of rafters. Treated as a beam, each rafter can be calculated according to accepted procedures for taking its share of the load. But how many and how far apart should the rafters be? A few large rafters far apart will be equivalent to many smaller rafters closer together. Thus the choice of how many versus how big becomes the design problem, which is decided on the basis of economics or aesthetics.

The results usually say how big, how thick, and so on, as a consequence of a design procedure and a choice. The collection of the results makes up the overall design.

Reviewing these criteria for design, it is apparent that the basis, assumptions, and specific conditions all combine to create a situation out of which grows a problem. The design procedure and choice similarly can be taken as the resolution of the problem, so that the results become information. The situation, problem, resolution, and information of thought classes thus become criteria for design. Furthermore, prose composition naturally progresses through stages, each of which takes all that went before as the situation for its unique problem, resolution, and information. Thus we have a reliable, established form through which prose composition can resemble design thinking.

Remembering that know-how is intellectual property that can be transferred only in the form of a service, and that a design embodies the completion of such a service, we see that a design represents a concrete method for transferring elusive intellectual property. If scientific and technical writing were given the same form as design, can such writing represent a surrogate method for transferring know-how? The answer lies in the nature of technical concepts, that occur both in design and in writing.

THE USE OF CONCEPTS

Despite the above extensive discussion of design thinking, the engineers who practice design rarely give much thought to their thinking. They tend to identify with the physical objects, which they hold in their minds by means of concepts. Because their concepts are so closely tied to reality, designers take the concepts to be real. To question a designer's concept is no less than blasphemy. Thus it is that when one engineer destroys a well-established concept, other engineers get excited. One such destruction had widespread effects and laid the groundwork for an experimental SPRI article, so that it offers a vivid, well-documented example.

The concept involved was that of fluid films. We live and breathe in the liquid and gaseous fluids water and air. We see all about us solid objects, ranging from window panes, to cooking pans, to water piping, to airplane surfaces, which move or hold those fluids in such ways that the exact nature of the contact between the fluid and the solid surface is extremely important. Technical people have experienced an urgent need for some concept through which they could characterize the fluid-solid contact, so that they could project phenomena along a smooth line from one condition to another. How much will a 4" pipe carry, compared to a 2"? Which will heat faster, boiling water or a frying steak? What will an aluminum trailer coating do to the gasoline consumption of the car that pulls the coated trailer through the air?

The concept of fluid films thinly coating the surfaces with which the fluid is in contact has allowed such projections in perhaps millions of examples. When we consider that this concept applies to the air in contact with a re-entering space vehicle, as well as the seawater in contact with an ocean-going vessel, as well as to the thousands of oils and chemicals that flow through pipes in refineries and chemical plants, we can see that the concept of fluid films is important.

One of the applications has been in the manufacture of ethylene, whose little molecule consists of two carbon atoms, each holding two hydrogen atoms, joined together by a double bond ($H_2C = CH_2$). Because it is little and because the double bond is chemically active, ethylene is used to make many other chemicals. And since ethylene is made from oil refinery products, its manufacture represents an important link between petroleum and chemicals. In that manufacture, the petroleum products are cracked at high temperatures, as they pass through pipes surrounded by intense flames.

You can see immediately, the role that fluid films must play along the inside of those pipes: Whatever the temperature in the center, the temperature will be higher in the film along the inside wall of the pipe. And since petroleum products crack all to way to carbon residue (coke) if the temperature is too high, there is a tendency for solid coke to form on the inside of the pipes of ethylene furnaces—sometimes so much as to plug those pipes.

This is exactly what has happened according to the concept of fluid films. And according to that concept, the maximum film temperature was related to a maximum heating rate—a heat flux of 12,000 Btus per hour per square foot of pipe surface. This maximum flux set the sizes of the furnaces required to produce a given amount of ethylene.

In the early 1960s, after much study of the supplies of petroleum feedstocks and the local markets, an East Coast refiner decided to build an ethylene plant near Philadelphia. After making inquiries, they commissioned the design of this plant to a New Jersey engineering company renowned for its know-how related to ethylene. That engineering company designed a plant incorporating the latest technology and supervised the construction. However, when it was time to bring the plant into production, it appeared that the furnaces were too small. The refiner complained to the engineering company, which responded by claiming that the furnaces were adequate if operated correctly. The refiner responded by hiring a well-known consultant to operate one side of one of the furnaces and challenged the engineering company to operate the other side of the same furnace.

Ethylene furnaces typically have a central brick wall down the middle, with the pipes lined up between both sides of that wall and many high-heat burners on the outsides. The piping connections outside the furnace are arranged so that any one in the line-up of pipes can be bypassed in case it cokes up solid.

The critical challenge-test operation came, with the consultant and his crew on one side of the furnace, and the crew from the engineering company operating the other. Operation was around the clock. As soon as a tube began to show signs of coke, the consultant reduced the firing rate to around 12,000 Btus per hour per square foot of pipe surface.

The engineering company's crew did likewise. But after a while, it became clear that this policy would show the furnace inadequate. The engineering company was responsible for the data used in the design, so that millions of dollars in replacements were at stake. Hours wore on, and the chief operating engineer from the engineering company stayed on duty. Finally, it appeared that both he and the furnace were about to give out, as another pipe showed signs of coking.

"Keep firing!" said the chief operating engineer, perhaps irrationally. That pipe coked up solid and was bypassed.

"Keep firing," said the engineer.

As might be expected, several more pipes soon showed signs of coking, but the chief operating engineer insisted that his crew keep firing at the design rate. Those pipes went too, and were bypassed, so that the furnace was reduced to less than half its quota of pipes. But the chief operating engineer kept firing that furnace at its full capacity.

Then a strange thing happened. The remaining pipes ceased to give any evidence of coke and operated smoothly, although they were now so hot that the steel of some of the pipes was softening, and the pipes were sagging in their supports. Even more remarkable, the yields of ethylene product were so much improved as to represent something new and different. The concept of film coking had been shattered.

Who says there is a fluid film? Nobody has ever seen one, or touched one, or measured its thickness. Although air currents above a wing are enough to support an airplane, and photos of re-entering space vehicles show them heated white hot on their surfaces from air friction, do those phenomena mandate a film of air over the surfaces of the objects? Ethylene manufacturers largely ignore the old concept of film coking in giant plants operating successfully around the world. Yet no adequate replacement for the concept of fluid films has been found.

Meanwhile, the changed concept of film coking altered other concepts of ethylene manufacture, and the renovated structure of concepts was described in a two-part report in *Chemical Week* magazine:

Heat flux and tube design: Reduced residence time is not a simple matter of speedup. The heat consumed by cracking hydrocarbons is fairly constant— about 5,100 Btu./lb. of ethylene when cracking ethane at 60% severity.

For cracking propane at 90% conversion, it's about 5,600 Btu./lb. of ethylene. Consequently, a shorter residence time requires that heat must be put into the hydrocarbons faster.

There are three ways to expand this heat input: (1) increase the proportion of steam to reduce the concentration of hydrocarbons in the furnace tubes; (2) alter the mechanical design of the tubes so they have a greater external surface per internal volume; (3) increase the rate of heat flow, or heat flux, through the furnace tube walls.

The cost of steam and the fact that throughput would be cut makes the first method uneconomical. The second solution is now being tried out at Daikowa Petrochemical with the Hercules-S&W design; a central core is put inside the cracking tubes to decrease the volume of hydrocarbons inside and increase the ratio of outside tube surface to volume of hydrocarbons. Otherwise the ratio of external tube surface to internal volume can be increased by reducing the tube diameter. But the third method is the approach believed to be that of Foster-Wheeler, Kellogg, Lummus and Selas. In fact, Lummus said it has increased the heat flux through the furnace tube walls to a level two or three times as great as the flux long deemed the maximum for steam cracking.

This article shows how the description of a problem (how to add more heat per unit of hydrocarbon per unit time) can be used to emphasize that problem's resolution (increased heat flux) that was based on a revised concept of fluid-film coking.

The importance of that revised concept is revealed in one consequence of the article. After publication, a large company approached one of the named engineering companies and ordered a $30 million ethylene plant incorporating the new design principles. The engineering company had not been in correspondence with the chemical company, and did not even know the chemical company was considering a new plant. Compared to the usual engineering contract, which is preceded by estimates and sales efforts costing as much as $1 million, the action on the part of the chemical company was stunning. The engineering company initiated an advertising campaign in which they offered free to prospective clients "black books" purported to give information on the company's other processes. However, none of those black books introduced concepts, and the advertising campaign failed.

The evidence of that example is supported by endless instances all showing that concepts are the distinguishing feature of writing on the professional level. A professional person who would write needs to know not only how to compose but also to understand concepts and their manipulation. It is essential for writing professionals to have an experience of concepts that goes beyond mere descriptions and involves their formation and application.

Unfortunately the notion of concepts, like the notion of design, is so familiar that most studies of concepts have had some purpose other than that of understanding concepts in principle. "The term concept is not the best-defined term in psychology," or anywhere else. The usual "experimental procedure, where a series of stimuli is presented and the subject responds to each, is fundamentally no different from the procedures used in discrimination, absolute judgment, or learning experiments."[1]

One exception to this observation might be worth describing for the insight gained from the imaginary experience. Imagine you are going through an experiment to examine how one forms concepts. You are seated at a table across from a person who will assist you in the experiment. On the table is a pile of blocks of many sizes, shapes, and colors. You are told that these blocks can be sorted into four groups, and that each of these four groups is identified by a symbol, either *lag*, *bik*, *mur*, or *cev*. But these symbols are always turned downward onto the table, so that you can not see them. You are to find out how quickly you can identify the characteristics of the symbols' four groups, with respect to color, shape, or size, without being able to see the identifying symbols. Altogether, there are twenty-two blocks. There are five different colors and six different shapes; some blocks are tall, some flat, some large, some small.

You begin by separating the blocks according to color, upon which your assistant picks up two blocks from two differently colored groups and, turning their bottoms to you, shows that they bear the same symbol. So it's not color. The blocks are pushed together again.

Again, you may assume that the groups are defined according to shapes (cubic, cylindrical, prismatic, etc.), and you may make a separation on that basis. Again your assistant picks up two blocks from two different groups and, turning their bottoms toward you, shows you that the two blocks carry the same symbol. So it's not shape either.

Obviously, your assistant knows something you do not know. Note how easily two blocks with identical names were chosen from your different groupings. Color and shape are the only variables with four or more kinds; your symbols must be associated with combinations of features. You begin more carefully, looking for four combinations of features that will account for all twenty-two blocks. Eventually, after some false starts, you notice that large blocks are associated with *lag* or *bik*, small ones with *mur* or *cev*. Then it comes to you: *lag* = large tall; *bik* = large flat; *mur* = small tall; and *cev* = small flat. With these four concepts, you can quickly separate the assembled blocks into their four groups, at a glance, as did your assistant.[2]

Although much simpler than many concepts, the formation of *lag*, *bik*, *mur*, and *cev* contains enough of the features of concept formation to be able to illustrate that process. It shows, first of all, two key characteristics:

- Concepts can only appear in response to strongly felt problems.
- Any concept must carry an identifying symbol, which can be a name (such as *lag*), a phrase (such as *regenerative clearcut*; *chondrocalcinosis*), or an extended phrase (such as *crude-oil heat-pickup train*).

In addition to these two attributes, concepts all have another distinguishing feature, well-known to designers, but often overlooked by psychologists.

—Every concept introduces its own characteristic problems.

It is this last feature that ties together thinking and writing on the professional level. For example, we return to the quote from the *Chemical Week* article, italicizing those concepts that generate their own problems to keep the thought flowing.

Heat flux and tube design: Reduced *residence time* is not a simple matter of speedup. The *heat consumed by cracking* hydrocarbons is fairly constant—about 5,100 Btu./lb. of ethylene when cracking at 60% severity.
For cracking propane at 90% conversion, it's about 5,600 Btu./lb. of ethylene. Consequently a shorter *residence time* requires that *heat* must be *put into* the hydrocarbons faster.
There are three ways to expand this *heat input*: (1) increase the proportion of steam to reduce the concentration of hydrocarbons in furnace tubes; (2) alter the mechanical design of the tubes so that they have greater external surface per internal volume; (3) increase the *rate* of *heat flow*, or *heat flux* through the tube walls.

It can be seen from reviewing this, as well as other texts, that the property of introducing problems changes concepts from dead-end solutions to a problem into sorts of ganglions through which problems entering from the direction of a previous concept are metamorphosed and sent off as new problems in search of yet another concept.

This property of acting as ganglions confers on concepts the ability to change a communication while carrying it along; and that leads to comparison between conceptual and logical thinking, such as was used under "Verbal Tools: Logic and Concepts" in the introduction to this book. In contrast to the metamorphoses taking place in communication through concepts, logic depends on deduction and inference, which can be traced to some form of metynomy or metaphor. Metonymy and metaphor can both be understood as composed of a tenor, a vehicle, and a ground: "The tenor of a metaphor is the object or idea we are talking about; the vehicle is the term to which the tenor is likened. The common element... is the ground."[3] Thus in the introduction to this book, one logical step was made within the progression of conceptual thinking about thermochemistry. A comparison of those ideas affords an example of the difference between conceptual and logical thinking and writing. The logical step was presented as: "Henry Le Chatelier (1885–1936) added the observation that a change in the conditions of a chemical system in equilibrium caused that system to react to accommodate the change."

This observation is actually a metaphor. Its tenor is the chemical equilibrium; its vehicle the push and pull of everyday life (water runs downhill; hot bodies cool off; gases under compression expand); and the common tendency to accommodate to the push and pull is the ground. Experiments to prove Le Chatelier's principle will have anticipated the result. Thus they will be biased, and they will lack the surprise and discovery that accompanies concept formation.

The manner in which a communication is metamorphosed in passing through a technical concept is further illustrated by the following examples. Take a concept, *modulus of elasticity*, as the unit stress required to produce a unit deformation in a material. We know that no material is infinitely elastic, so the concept *modulus of elasticity* leads to the problem: What do we call that unit stress required to produce unit deformation beyond the elastic limit of the material? The concept of a measurable *creep strength*, which comes from the property of metal crystals to adjust to super elastic stresses by sliding over each other, is commonly used for metals in high temperature service. Again, take the concept, *heat flux*, that was used in the *Chemical Week* article. This has been described as the units of heat passing through unit surface per unit time. But this does not take into consideration temperature; and everyone knows by observation that the rate at which heat passes through a surface is dependent on the temperature difference on the two sides of that surface. So what is the basis for the concept of *heat flux*? Two concepts, *radiation* and *convection*, which both take place on the ethylene furnace's pipes. The radiation from the burners of the furnace to the outside surface of the pipes varies with the fourth power of the temperatures; the convective heat transfer is directly proportional to the difference in temperature between the metal pipe and the fluid inside. The concept of heat flux is used as a simplification for the overall rate with similar pipes, in order to avoid calculating both radiation and convection by trial and error.

Of course, the development of an original concept is relatively rare among professionally trained individuals, and for the most part the concepts of a profession are learned the same way as lay concepts are. Take, for example, a book. If you close that book and hold it to a toddling child just learning to speak, saying, "book," the child may, after some repetition, make the association and sometime later say, "book," while indicating the same book. However, it would be wrong to assume that the child has a concept of "book." The name is knows is limited through association with only one book and possibly with the one person holding that book. A few years later, that association will have expanded to include variously bound volumes separately from the people holding those volumes. However, this will still be only a name for a generalization; and it is only in adult thinking that the true, abstract, stable, flexible, articulate, discrete, and definite concept of "book" will have become identified with a collection of thoughts leading to one or more principles, such as the different books of the Christian Bible.

The development of most professional concepts is parallel with this development of the concept of "book." Students are coerced into memorizing the fundamental concepts, which they carry in their minds as names. It is only after they experience the application of those names in solving a problem that they come into possession of the concept symbolized by the name.

Thus concepts are the units of thought through which both design thinking and SPRI prose follow a purpose toward a goal, the thread of thought passing through repeated metamorphoses, as it traverses each concept. Consequently, the next stage of our search for clear writing consists of understanding that metamorphosis. This is closely related to the problem.

APPLIED PROBLEMS

The development and application of concepts by means of a problem was demonstrated through an interview with Dr. Alex Oblad, then director of research at the M. W. Kellogg Company. The idea was to carry out the interview for purposes of obtaining insights into industrial research, and later to find a "newshook" to justify an article that used those insights. Dr. Oblad had been described as a man with *charism*, a word I mistrusted but was to learn about.

The interview took place mid-morning at Dr. Oblad's office in New York, with the understanding between the public relations man and me that I would finish before lunch and that he and I would compare notes over lunch. It began politely and moved to a broad discussion of the importance of research and the different kinds of research. After a full hour of this conversation, by my watch, it began to appear that nothing would result from the interview. So I explained that, although the conversation was pleasant, it was not what I sought. My purpose in the interview was to obtain enough understanding to write a competent article. Citing Ernest Hemingway's metaphor of the writer's intellectual iceberg, I explained that in technical writing the ratio of things known to things written was often much higher than seven to one. Because of this, it was my policy as a reporter to treat everything in strict confidence until I had cleared the actual writing with the source; and although I retained my right to my own interpretation, I would allow any source to strike his or her confidential material from any draft.

Dr. Oblad stared at me for a second or two. "All right," he decided and sat back in his chair. "My budget is X millions. Here's how I justify it."

And then, matter-of-factly, with complete confidence in my promise of confidentiality, he explained his approach to research. This began with an assumption that any commercially viable process would have to be given its final tests in a pilot plant that operated around the clock. This required a minimum crew of shift workers. Because he preferred to treat this crew as permanent employees, it immediately became apparent that they would be able to handle a few pilot plant projects per year, operating year around. This set a continuous demand for a laboratory and chemists capable of first testing the projects in glassware on laboratory benches; it also set a demand for metallurgists, chemical engineers, and so forth, to make the transition from glass to the pilot plant equipment; and it also set a demand for theoretical chemists to originate process ideas to be tested in the glassware.

As Dr. Oblad completed this organizational sketch, he leaned forward and, with a flattened hand held above his desk, scrubbed it around as if erasing something.

"Now, what does all this theory mean?" he said. "Nothing!" And he leaned further forward for emphasis. "I've got but one job here, and that is to keep those people solving important problems. We've got some of the best people in the world, but those best people are worth no more than the problems they solve. And it's up to me to see that the problems they work on are important."

How to do that? In the answer, as he gave it, a review of Dr. Oblad's research budget showed that a minimum of so many commercially viable processes had to be invented each year to justify that budget. This meant that a minimum percentage of the few pilot plant projects must be successful. In order to achieve this statistical quality, experience dictated that another, larger number of worthwhile processes must be investigated in the laboratory. And in order to achieve that number of worthwhile processes for laboratory investigation, experience further dictated that another, still larger number of promising new processes must be provided by the theoretical chemists. Over it all was a group of specialized economic evaluators who reviewed each process at each step along its progress to the pilot plant.

Thus Dr. Oblad added data in the form of numbers of specific jobs, based on experience and statistics, to match the conceptual structure of his research organization. Those data represented answers to the functional problem of keeping his people busy on important problems. Without the conceptual structure the numbers of jobs meant nothing. Conversely, a recitation of the conceptual structure of the organization meant little without the data.

Analogous situations are confronted throughout the professional literature, where published information remains effectively proprietary for lack of its complementary data or concepts. For example, I have found the same numbers of chemists, metallurgists, ceramicists, and so on, listed for M. W. Kellogg in a book on research organizations in the United States; and descriptions of ideal research organizations similar to his can be found elsewhere in the technical literature. In this way, the interview with Dr. Oblad shows clearly how concepts and data attain mutual value by association through a problem and its resolution.

Accordingly, the expression of problem/resolution, whether written or stated, divides both prose composition and real life events into a problem side called the situation, and a resolution-side, called the information. Such a division leads to questions about what causes some thinking to be part of a situation while other thinking is part of the information. Information has been shown, through information-theory studies, to be the opposite equal to uncertainty; and thinking that leads to a problem might be contributing to uncertainty. Does information represent the opposite equal to situation? No, because the resolution can act as a concept to metamorphose the thinking to suit the problem. Does this mean that some of the thinking of a situation merely needs a suitable problem to become significant data? Yes. How might one further describe the differences between situation and information?

Situation and information are formally identical but functionally different, in the manner of a piece of glass that can be a mirror, a window, or a writing surface, depending on how it is used. Numerous experiences in editing technical articles showed that almost any given thought could be designated either as situation or as information, depending on the choice of the problem and its resolution. Sometimes the different functions may be signalled by words. For example, many legal contracts contain a preamble consisting of "whereas" clauses, which serve to set the situation for a statement of a problem and resolution that identify the purpose of the contract and the functions of all the clauses to follow. For another example, a friend from one of the engineering companies remarked that their pilot plant manager once objected that requested data had been available for a long time. Perhaps, but the designers had not conceived of the problem to make that old data useful. Again, the introduction of this book cites several books thirty years old or older that may have been overlooked and forgotten because they came before the time of the problems they solve.

Because a writer can choose a problem and its resolution, it is possible to direct the reader's attention to information that might otherwise be overlooked. The wide choice available for problem/resolution is illustrated by a report from a press conference involving a new ammonia process that had achieved phenomenal success and has since affected the world supplies of food and fertilizers. At the time of the press conference, the first three dozen plants using the process had just been built. Some of those plants had experienced difficulties in achieving full operating capacity. The engineering company that had invented the process and built those plants wanted to publicize the difficulties and prove that the causes had been eliminated, in order to dispel the fears of prospective new clients. The purpose of the press conference was to describe the difficulties and what had been done about them.

This was an unusually esoteric press conference. Only five reporters were invited, from five leading trade journals of the chemical and fertilizer industries. There were no press releases and no speeches. Instead, there were photocopies of references and pages of data available for the taking. And the five reporters were matched by as many experts on ammonia plant design. The mood of the conference was basically that of a symposium. Since each of the reporters had already written at least one article about this ammonia process, explanations were sophisticated and to the point.

The principal point made by the engineering company was that, despite the admitted difficulties, the new ammonia plants had lost only 15 percent of their operating time for adjustments during the first months of operation. This was acceptable for any new plant and good for a new process; but it did not respond to any questions about the specific difficulties. There were more than five of those difficulties, which had occurred repeatedly, been studied, and were resolved. But these were scattered over the process randomly without any unifying theme, so that an attempt to discuss them in any order would be discursive. How could a reporter put all this together in a short article that would both provide the information and be easy to read?

The answer demonstrates the flexibility of choice possible with the resolution thought. Instead of being a concept or a thematic part of the technology, the resolution chosen for that article was a flow sheet of the ammonia process, on which the start-up difficulties were located and identified by key words, such as *silica migration* or *high-speed gears*. A problem leading to that illustration-as-resolution was a simple statement of the most provocative question: What, exactly, had been the start-up problems? A situation leading to that problem was the disclosure that the down-time during start-up was 15 percent. The information became descriptions of the difficulties and their solutions, keyed to the flow sheet through the key words.

The acceptance of that article was remarkable, not only for an article on a well-documented subject like ammonia, but for articles in general. The readership rating was high; there were many favorable comments; and a few months after it appeared, a design engineer from a competing engineering company said that the article had been studied carefully by specialists, and he remarked on the knowledge shown by the article.

This incident thus reveals not only one way to compose an article but also a means for inverting Hemingway's iceberg, so that the apparent knowledge is more than the actual. The know-how for the design of ammonia plants is vast. Few people command that know-how. Yet an article that brought together random aspects of the ammonia process and discussed each of those with sophistication gave the impression that all the non-discussed aspects were understood equally well. This impression applies to most articles that use an illustration-as-resolution; and it also carries over to what the reader feels he or she gets out of the article, and thus accounts for the consistently high readership ratings for such articles, relative to the popularity of their subjects.

Once discovered, that illustration-as-resolution method of composition came to be used so frequently that it could be called a technique. Each time it brought similar successful results. The application to patent studies even became a sub-type. Many times, the numbers of patents studied for researching a technical article would come to more than twenty, sometimes more than 100. Usually, most of those patents would be pertinent, but not related by any theme, so that there was some need for tying them together. There was always a desire to account for time spent studying the patents by referring to those patents. Also, since it is against the law to lie in a patent disclosure (but not to reporters) the data presented in those disclosures were reliable. How to bring all that good data, plus the pertinent patents to the attention of readers in a form that they could easily grasp? Time and again, published articles showed that if, as with ammonia, the patents were identified by number on some sort of flow sheet of unit operations it was possible to make sense out of otherwise disparate data. This technique made it possible to publish the results of almost any patent search, because the situation was always bits of varied news about activity in the field; the problem was a statement about the technical complexity; the resolution was the illustration, where everything was brought together; and the information became a discussion of the different patents keyed to the flow sheet by number. This type of article was used for reporting developments in nylon, urea, and oxychlorination, among other fields. In another instance, illustration-as-resolution was used to describe so-called critical path scheduling; and again, it was used to compare delivery times (thus construction delays) for equipment purchased in different countries.

A careful choice of problem/resolution can enable us to string concepts along a metamorphosing thread of thought toward an objective. How does one go about choosing that objective? How does a string of concepts come to make a good design?

SPRI AND DESIGN THINKING

During the first experiments in editing according to SPRI, one article came to serve as a pattern for many subsequent articles. While skimming through a stack of papers that had recently been delivered at a meeting of mechanical engineers, I happened onto one of those rare instances in which an engineering company divulged the sort of design information usually kept confidential. This engineering company specialized in the design of large brick-lined reactors, on the order of 8 feet in diameter by 60 feet tall, such as are used to make wood into paper. The technical paper, written by a vice president of that company, presented the tortuous calculation procedure for those reactors, as it progressed through nearly twenty pages. I wrote the author asking for permission to edit that paper for publication. He answered, granting permission within a few days.

When approached with SPRI in mind, that technical paper revealed a form that has turned out to be almost classic for inexperienced professionals writing for the first time. In a brief introduction, the author stated that the design of brick-lined reactors was complicated, and that the best way to describe how to do it was probably just to start at the beginning of the calculations. With that, he began with number 1, and described that step in a couple paragraphs; then he proceeded through the whole sequence of numbered calculation steps, describing each in one or more paragraphs. As a consequence, the technical paper read somewhat like many cookbooks.

According to SPRI, the first step in editing that article was to discover a central problem and its resolution to which the rest of the information could be subservient. Somewhere near the middle of the calculation sequence, it was brought out that the reactor had to be designed for atmospheric pressure and temperature as well as for operating conditions of several hundreds of pounds pressure and degrees temperature. Between these two sets of conditions, the brick lining expanded or contracted at different rates from the vessel's steel shell. If the lining were too thin, the bricks would come loose and fall out at ambient conditions; if the lining were too thick or too tightly fitted, its inner surface would be overstressed and crack at operating conditions. Furthermore, the steel shell needed to be strong enough to contain both the operating pressure inside the vessel and the expansion pressure of the lining, while the lining needed to be thick enough to resist the action of the chemicals inside the vessel. The only way to arrive at a design of lining-plus-shell was by trial and error, each set of calculations beginning with assumptions in step 1, and proceeding to calculated values of the assumed proportions in the final step. Then the calculated values were compared to the assumptions and the whole cycle repeated until they matched.

In the original paper, the notions of differential expansion and contraction were associated with individual calculation steps. I identified them with the problem, and the first assumptions of the trial-and-error cycle as its resolution. All thoughts that modified those two were lifted from various positions among the numbered steps, and grouped accordingly. The result was a brief situation that stated the subject of the article, followed by relatively long discussions of the problem and resolution. The numbered calculation steps, which had shrunk to bare recitations, then followed as information. The edited article was sent to the author for approval and published. Shortly after publication, the author wrote me a letter saying that the experience had been unusually rewarding for him. No one but the two of us seemed to recognize that the conference paper and the article contained identical thoughts.

By appearing first as the conference paper, that article made possible a number of observations about plagiarism and proprietary know-how, about the writing of average professionals, and about readers. The article was so much a type that it became the forerunner of a practice of screening technical conferences for superior papers that could be edited into articles for magazine publication. The thoughts of those conference papers were usually so disorganized that it was always possible to avoid reproducing more than 100 consecutive words of the original text. Thus, although permission was always obtained from the technical societies, it might have been legally possible to plagiarize the papers without such permission. More important, the edited articles were taken as original material, even though every thought was accounted for in the conference papers, the one exception being the statement of the problem. In nearly a dozen instances, the author neglected to articulate the problem answered in the text. In fact, when presented with problem thoughts in the edited versions for review, the authors had a tendency to claim "no problem!" even when it was explained that the problem had been answered.

Comparisons between the conference papers and the published articles were interesting. Readers who had been exposed to both did not seem to associate the two. Some authors tended to identify so strongly with the thoughts they had put in the original papers that they took both the original and edited versions as the same; other authors seemed to feel a sense of loss, as if something had been taken from them in the edited version. Most importantly, editing those papers showed how technical writing might possibly transmit know-how in the manner that a designer transmits know-how in the form of a service. Typically, the original papers dealt with esoteric calculation procedures; the author simply plunged right into the calculation and described it. Consequently, none of the conference papers put the calculation into perspective, so that the usefulness of those papers was limited to people who already knew how to put the procedures to work in an overall design, that is to people already in possession of the prerequisite know-how. However, the mere statement of a problem with its resolution succeeded in putting the calculation procedure into a context whereby it could be used flexibly in a stable procedure. The example of the brick-lined reactor was typical. The original paper presented that calculation method as good for the case of brick-lined reactors only. However, when it was given perspective with its problem and resolution, that calculation method became a procedure useful for any case of a cylindrical vessel with composite walls. There are many such vessels, so that the procedure has widespread application. It thus gained flexibility through an objective rationality; and it came to represent know-how.

Thus a professional who writes has the choice of merely following an established sequence or of searching out a problem that will bring out the general significance of the technology, and will relate that technology conceptually to other technologies. In articulating those problems, the writer is actually engaging in prose design. As in all design, the written expression of problem/resolution divides the thinking into a problem-side and a resolution-side, called situation and information, respectively.

Comparisons with design and writing give many illustrations for the parts of SPRI composition. We can begin to regard those parts as tools that have discrete characteristics and functions. We know what they are and how they are related. It remains to figure out what it is that enables them to function as they do, so that we are best able to use them. That concern leads us to the concept of *feedback*.

FEEDBACK FOR CHAPTER 2

This chapter began with the observation that instructions for writing must come to terms with thinking, which poses a problem because of the complexity of thought. That problem is resolved by taking design procedure as the standard for prose composition, as well as for design. Design thinking was examined through an example of refinery design, and found to be composed of six criteria: a basis, assumptions, specific conditions, a problem, a procedure, and results. These were combined into the four parts of SPRI prose composition: situation, problem, resolution, and information.

The similarity between design and SPRI composition led to a search for the means that might enable prose composition to act like design. The answer was that such means can be found in concepts, which are common to both writing and design. The concept of fluid films, along with its application in ethylene pyrolysis, were used to demonstrate the importance of technical concepts.

The observation that concepts are not generally understood and consciously experienced led to a description of a psychological test in concept formation. This test showed that concepts have three properties: they can only appear in response to a strongly felt problem; they must have an identifying symbol; and they each introduce new problems of their own. These three properties led to a description of conceptual thinking as a sequential activity in which the thought is metamorphosed as it passes through each concept of the sequence. The ability of problems to control the changing thread of conceptual thinking led to the question of how to discover problems.

The description of an interview with Dr. Oblad was used to show how a managerial problem of research administration gave significance to the make-up of a research company. The interview illustrated how problems give significance to data. The range of situations through which this is true was demonstrated with an example of an article written about the start-up difficulties of ammonia plants. It was shown that almost anything can be the source of a problem, and that the careful articulation of a problem can direct the thoughts of conceptual thinking. That observation led to the question of identifying useful problems. This led to a comparison of SPRI composition and design thinking.

The experience of editing conference papers for magazine publication was used to show how professionals who were inexperienced writers tended to describe only calculation procedures without articulating a problem to put those procedures into perspective. The proper perspective for such papers is given by describing the general design problem that the calculation procedure is used in. Accordingly, a writer might be able to perform a service and transmit know-how by articulating a design problem and its answer. That notion led to the question of how situations, problems, resolutions, and information are able to act as they do, which brought us to this example of feedback.

The concept of feedback can be illustrated in terms of perception, through a description of the action-produced perceptions of sight, smell, hearing, and so on.

Action-produced stimulation is obtained, not imposed—that is, obtained by the individual, not imposed on him. It is intrinsic to the flow of activity, not extrinsic to it; dependent on it, not independent of it. Instead of entering the nervous system through receptors, it re-enters. The input is not merely afferent, in the terminology of the neurologists, but re-afferent—that is, contingent on efferent output. The favorite modern term for this action-produced input is one borrowed from electronic circuitry, namely, feedback.[4]

Although the concept of feedback had to wait until after World War II for neurologists and electronics theorists to give it articulation, designers have for centuries obtained action-produced information by comparing results calculated toward a purposeful choice. Without this kind of feedback, design does not exist. Any design represents a purposeful choice; without that choice there is no design, only a calculation; and a choice mandates feedback.

In designing distillation towers, such as those of the Bordeaux refinery, each tower is sized to handle a reflux of overhead product returned to the top tray, as well as to contain the number of trays required to make a separation between products. If the reflux is increased, the required number of trays is reduced; and if the number of trays is increased, the required reflux is reduced. Between the limits of complete reflux and infinite trays there is an optimum. The distillation-tower designer calculates reflux and trays, but chooses the optimum.

Similarly, in designing ethylene furnaces, each set of pipes in every furnace is calculated to receive a given amount of heat while transferring the reacting hydrocarbons. Narrow pipes will increase the heat-receiving surface relative to the volume of hydrocarbons, and vice versa. Complete calculations are made for several diameters of pipes, and the designer chooses an optimum, which makes allowance for pressure drop through the pipes, residence time in the pipes, and amount of heat received. Again, the design is a choice.

By the same token, a brick-lined reactor need not be 8 feet in diameter by 60 feet tall. There is an infinite number of combinations of diameters and heights possible for the given volume. Consequently the designer of brick-lined reactors, or any cylindrical vessel, must do calculations for various combinations of length-to-diameter and eventually choose an optimum.

Design of roof supports for a house mandates a choice between many small rafters or fewer large rafters. That design, like all designs, is a choice. Choice mandates comparison. Comparison mandates feedback.

Most revealing of all, perhaps, is the nature of the choice underlying the design of Dr. Oblad's research organization. Readers unfamiliar with design may have been misled to understand a fixed budget for that organization when Dr. Oblad said, "All right, my budget is X millions, here's how I justify it." What if that budget were either increased or decreased? On the one hand, more back-up staff could be added to the pilot plant in order to increase statistical quality; on the other hand, the back-up facilities could be reduced until nothing but the pilot plant remained. This second alternative, which leads to a considerable sacrifice in statistical quality of the research work, does represent the research efforts of many engineering companies, whose pilot plants serve only to amass data for proprietary processes. Considering the possibilities, it becomes apparent that Dr. Oblad's "justification" represented an optimum, so that his answer to the problem of keeping his people busy solving important problems was more than merely a balance; it was an optimum administrative design for process research in the chemical industry.

When we've learned to ask ourselves what is best, when we've learned to see complex analyses as test solutions in a trial-and-error search, when we understand the role of feedback in comparing results from many specific analyses, while adjusting the goal; then we have arrived at a comprehension of design as it applies in the real world, and as it is practiced by most professionally trained people.

Obviously, this kind of design is complicated, particularly in instances where the specific analyses may also be trial and error, so that there is trial and error within trial and error. The problem is more than the human mind can hold. We need some sort of notation that will enable us to keep track of our thinking. Ideally, this notation should be familiar to us; it should be rigorous; it should be something we can dissect and analyze, so that we can manipulate it consciously; and it should be readily understood by others.

Many computer programs and mathematical systems have been proposed for this purpose, but I suggest to you language—the English language you use naturally. There is no need to change it or to modify it in any way. It is all there, fully adequate to the capacity of your mind and the design tasks you may undertake. It can operate either in the lightning-fast primitive mode of thought, or be calculatedly conscious through chains of concepts. It carries within it all the requirements for concept formation and promulgation. It also carries the concepts. It is adapted to the rise and fall of uncertainties, as they appear and are resolved in transforming situation into information. And it is immediately recognizable by your peers. Furthermore, even if your peers have not mastered your common language to the extent that you have, they will accept without objection your most complicated and sophisticated uses of the language, as long as you do it properly.

PROCEDURE FOR PROSE COMPOSITION

Assume that you are to create, through thinking, a prose composition. You should achieve the following criteria:

1. Establish a subject, an audience interested in that subject, and a reason for that interest.
2. Discover a problem related to the established interest, and think up a resolution that answers the problem and bears on the established subject.
3. Outline facts and data to describe the situation from which the problem arises, as well as to support the resolution.
4. Feedback the results of steps 3, 2, and 1, while adjusting those results to better suit each other and the purpose of the composition.

Before attempting this approach, you might want to consider an alternative. In the November 23, 1986, issue of *The New York Times Book Review*, accomplished writer Nora Ephron explains that, because she "types like the wind," she creates a composition by writing many successive drafts, starting each successive draft from the beginning and retyping and rewriting the previous draft up to the point where it left off, then continuing from that point as far as she can under a sort of momentum. Her flowing compositions, which are the best proof of her method, represent journeys of discovery through thoughts on paper. They lead to highly creative associations of language and thought. If you can type that fast, or if you have a dictating machine, you can almost certainly benefit from trying her method; and if you do try it, you may make an interesting discovery.

In the manner that a mountain range divides rainfall into two separate watersheds, the decision to begin a composition with either words or thoughts will cause the subsequent composition to assume one of two distinct patterns. Language-dominated prose, which results from Ephron's method, has been explored for centuries by many great writers; and it has been thoroughly analyzed by students of literature. However, language-dominated prose is not suited to expressing new concepts or discoveries, when they occur outside the thought patterns already established between the language and its culture. Therefore language-dominated prose tends to be easier to read and to bypass more complicated subjects, whereas thought-dominated prose is more difficult, not only because its subjects are more difficult but also because it passes over fluid expressions in favor of precision. This confronts the thoughtful writer with the problem of discovering some method beyond language for making his or her prose interesting and rewarding. The most obvious way to do this is to shape the written thoughts to fit a specific interest carried by the reader—step 1 in our procedure for composition.

Step 1: Establish Audience, Subject, and Interest

Most professionally trained people assume that they have a rapport with others who have undergone the same training. However, a bit of reflection will show that this rapport is rarely as complete as is imagined. A walk past the meeting rooms at a national conference for any large society will show that some of those rooms are almost empty while others are full to overflowing. What causes those differences in attendance? Unfortunately, a deliberate comparison of papers given to large and small audiences has failed to reveal any distinct patterns to explain the difference in interest. Audiences have left crowded meeting rooms feeling disappointed, and empty rooms feeling rewarded. In either case the audience reaction comes too late for planning the composition of the paper. It is necessary to look beyond prose composition to discover clues to audience interest.

The best way to deal with this problem is to discover how it is approached by the large professional journals that depend on advertising for most of their income. The survival of such journals depends on their ability to demonstrate that they can interest their subscribers; they must prove to advertisers that not only are they read by a requisite number of authoritative professionals, but also that those readers are interested in the journal. Because subscription costs are often less than the cost of publication, professional journals generally follow some sort of procedure for restricting subscribers. Among other things, subscribers are required to indicate their positions or titles on the subscription application; and the numbers of subscribers with specific titles are reported to the advertisers. A typical list of titles might include the following:

company executives
financial and legal staff
consulting-company staff
independent consultants
plant foremen and superintendents
technical staff
research staff
professors
students

This list might apply to any one of a number of industrial professions. Furthermore, it is apparent that individuals with the same title or position might have as much or more in common than individuals with the same professional training. Rather than to assume an interested audience, therefore, an author should learn to identify specific interests in terms of both profession and function. Although this exercise may be discouraging, one should remember that the editors who review your article would have been conditioned to question the article's interest along such lines. Also, because your article is flexible at this point, you can easily adjust your subject, allow a tentative answer, and proceed to step 2.

Step 2: State the Problem and Its Resolution

If you are typical, you approached the notion of composing an article with the idea that you have something special to offer. Now, explore the possibilities for a resolution that will put your something special into perspective and lend it significance. This is a creative endeavor difficult to describe other than in terms of the notions offered earlier in this chapter. Bear in mind the notion of feedback, and compare several partially defined resolutions against your prior answers to audience interest. When one resolution seems to suit better than the others, see how easily you can find a problem for it. When you've arrived at a tentative combination of problem/resolution, move on to step 3.

Step 3: Assemble Facts for the Situation and Information

If you are typical, you will have approached the notion of an article with some facts to back up what you feel you have to say. You need to ask how well your tentative resolution adds significance to those facts, and how well that added significance corresponds to what you hoped to say. If you do not have facts on hand, you have probably gone off course somewhere and need to review steps 1 and 2. Then you have to adjust the misfit.

If your facts do fit, you are well on the way to a composition, with audience, resolution, problem, and information all identified. The next step is to review the general field with your intended audience in mind, in order to choose the situation for description. A situation will always be available, once a suitable combination of problem, resolution, and information has been discovered. With the situation identified, move on to step 4.

Step 4: Feedback

Up to this point, you can have done your composing mentally and quickly. Now, however, you will need to slow down and make written notes. List the following:

- Your audience, its interest, and the reason for that interest
- The problem that relates this interest to a resolution
- The resolution
- The sources of the information
- The situation that gives rise to the audience's interest

Repeat the four-step procedure until all parts of the composition seem destined for each other. At that point, your composition is complete. Either write the article or proceed to Chapter 3.

Example. A short article written under the pen name, A. R. Chimes, can serve as an example for this procedure. This article appeared to get the highest readership rating of all the articles written or edited for *Chemical Engineering*.

I had been assigned a section of the magazine called "Plant Notebook," which published, every second issue, several short articles describing discoveries or ideas recently evolved by readers in the course of their work. This was a pleasant assignment. Many of the ideas were clever; some were technically elegant. Over the years, more and more readers responded to the tone of the articles, so that the section became one of the magazine's most popular, with an ever growing list of suggestions for more articles.

Many of the suggestions represented a short-cut to a routine calculation or a novel approach to a common problem, of the sort that young engineers a few years out of school discover during the course of their work. Although these often repeated known principles, they carried a contagious fascination for the work that seemed to encourage others. Many concerned methods for determining the required sizes of pipes; and a number of those were nomographs. Unfortunately some of the published nomographs contained errors.

Readers were quick to catch these errors. Most of the readers wrote about them in a spirit of cooperative correction. However, there was a professor in a metropolitan technical school who was a self-appointed specialist on pipe sizing; and he began checking all the Plant Notebook articles in detail. More of those than I like to confess did contain errors, and the professor found occasion to write letters of complaint. I refused to take the time to make careful technical checks of nomographs and charts, but began to be afraid he would complain to the editor-in-chief. There had to be some way to get rid of that professor.

At this point, let's consider our four-step composition procedure. The audience was fixed. It included many young company engineers, and staff engineers, as well as professors, students, and consultants. The subject was pipe sizing. The specific reasons for interest were involved with the speed and accuracy of the sizing methods. The desired article should speak to all of the audience and divert the audience's attention away from a preoccupation with accuracy.

Fortunately, I had in my files some old charts that had been used to size many miles of piping in operating plants; and those charts avoided meticulous academic calculations. Those charts became the resolution. The problem then needed was some sort of question that would cast doubt on the academic methods and emphasize the utility of the charts. A paraphrase of the published article follows. The thought classes, shown in italics, were not published.

Situation. Perhaps no area of chemical engineering technology is so much studied and documented as pipe sizing. In addition to the dimensionless Reynolds number, there are equations by Fanning and Darcy, as well as correlations for optimum economic pipe sizes.

Problem. Unfortunately, the careful application of all these correlations often borders on the ridiculous, for the simple reason that the person who sizes a pipe usually does not know how long it is. In order to know the lengths of the piping, it is necessary to have the plant laid out and all the equipment items located in space. However, the sizes of the piping are a major consideration in locating equipment for minimum piping runs and minimum piping cost, so that it is necessary to size the piping in order to lay out the plant.

Resolution. For this reason, design engineering companies that design whole plants routinely size the piping by approximate correlations based on experience. Two charts showing such correlations are shown above. On these charts are indicated "confidence lines" used to size a pipe according to whether it is a pump discharge, pump suction, or a gravity flow of boiling liquid.

Information. The charts were discussed in some detail.

After publication of that article, the professor stopped pestering me, and the submissions of pipe sizing correlations dropped off dramatically. The readership survey showed that the acceptance of the article was outstanding.

The composition of that article also demonstrated the use of SPRI composition as an aid to clear thinking. I had worked on the design of many plants, for which approximate correlations were used not only to specify pipe sizes, but also heat-exchanger pressure drops, pump-pressure differentials, control-valve pressure drops, and so on. However, I had never given thought to the true function of those approximate correlations, which is to simplify the trial-and-error process of whole-plant design. The need to articulate the problem for the resolution offered by those old charts then forced me to perceive that pipe sizing and plant layout must be trial-and-error procedures.

With that example, we come to the end of the discussion of SPRI prose composition. The next concern is the organization of individual thoughts and concepts within the SPRI classes. This is the subject for Chapter 3.

3

WORDS THAT SHARE

INTRODUCTION TO CHAPTER 3: USES OF UNCERTAINTY

This chapter fulfills the promise, made in Chapter 1, to present "explicit instructions on how to ... assemble thoughts for easy and interesting reading." That fulfilled promise is accompanied by some notions picked up in Chapters 1 and 2. Among those is the notion that professional people do considerable thinking beyond the thinking they normally express by speaking and writing. Evidence of this notion has been available for years in legal case records, graphs, mathematical formulae, computer programs, and creatively designed objects, all of which give evidence of thought that is not expressed in words and sentences. Yet almost all treatises on English composition assume, like the French writer Nicolas Boileau-Despereaux (1636–1711), that that which is well understood is clearly expressed, as well as the converse, that that which is poorly expressed is poorly understood.

This false assumption represents an occupational hazard to professional people working in research, law, teaching, and similar fields, who endanger their careers when they prepare poorly written briefs, reports, and compendiums. Although other professionals, like designers and engineers, can point to their work as physical evidence of their ability, they also suffer in comparison with peers more adept at prose. Consequently, all professionals can benefit by improving the skill with which they translate their thoughts into clear writing.

However, it is extremely difficult to consciously acquire such skills. The problem lies in the elusiveness of non-verbal thought. Nearly always, non-verbal thoughts are expressed through the medium of some activity, even such a simple activity as classifying and filing documents, using a telephone, or choosing clothes to wear for the day. Because such activities are performed without even the silent egocentric speech studied by psychologists, the act of ordering up words to express the thoughts in the absence of the actions is difficult; and the act of organizing and arranging those words so that they are easily understood by others is difficult indeed.

Although the ease with which many writers appear to match words to thoughts might seem to belie this difficulty, a closer look at facile writing reveals something different. Exactly because they do believe writing and thought are synonomous, commercial writers do not undertake the problem of putting words to specific non-verbal thoughts. Instead they adapt the thought to the words. A summary review of literature shows that novelists begin with a story and alter the facts to make the story convincing, whereas a professional person who writes must alter the prose to convince readers of the facts. Similarly, essayists begin with a well-turned phrase and build on that. Typically, John begins: "In the beginning was the Word; and the Word was with God; and the Word was God" (John 1:1). And then he proceeds to write the fourth Gospel of the New Testament.

What is needed is some way to consciously attach words to the wordless thought that serves otherwise only to direct our actions—some sort of bridge that will transport known words into that wordless world and back. With this device, it should be possible to take hold of non-verbal thoughts and set them to words. Such a device has been suggested by an arbitrary analogy with mathematical measurements of uncertainty.[1] Information theory complemented by a method of multivariate analysis is used to make numerical measurements of such things as the appeal of a patterned design or a musical melody; and the measurements are then confirmed by the results of psychological tests. These systems arrive at a partitioning of meaning; they show how the total meaning can be divided into an internal part and an external part. These internal and external parts are joined by an expression whose meaning is described as "signification."

According to arbitrary analogy, the English language possesses an external structure specific to it and capable of meaning. English words can also symbolize ideas and things that are parts of an internal, non-verbal thought structure, also capable of meaning. The words that symbolize an idea or thing have significance in terms of that symbol and hence signification for the non-verbal thought structure.

Now, our purpose in making this analogy is to discover if there is some relation between verbal and non-verbal thought. If the analogy is good, some of the rules of the mathematical constructs should also apply to the relations between prose and non-verbal thinking—rules such as the following:

1. *The meaning content of a non-verbal thought system depends on the number of its variables.*
    Practically, this means that we must learn to identify the degrees of uncertainty possible for a thought system, and to adapt the complexity of our prose to that.
2. *The total meaning of the verbal and non-verbal system is constant.*
    Practically, this means that, in order to translate thoughts into clear prose, we must learn to match the content of the prose to the content of the thought system. We can not depend on implication and suggestion to make do for a simple statement, nor can we extend a simple thought with extravagant statements.
3. *Redundancy in the verbal part of the system tends to reduce the meaning content of the verbal part, as the non-verbal part is increased proportionately.*
    Practically, this means that redundancy does not advance the thought.

These rules seem reasonable and simple, provided we can follow rule 1 and identify the degrees of uncertainty possible for a thought system. This has been done. And the proof of our analogy has been that it works. It has transformed a vague problem into a search for specific uncertainty that can be used to give verbal form to inarticulate thoughts. Uncertainty and how to identify it thus becomes the focal point in the search for explicit instructions on how to assemble thoughts for easy and interesting reading. This chapter will deal first with sources of uncertainty, then those sources will be taken individually, so as to identify possible degrees of uncertainty in each source, and finally, these will be brought together for explicit instructions.

SOURCES OF UNCERTAINTY

Uncertainty and its mirror image, information, have been central to a large quantity of empirical studies of perception,[2,3] as well as to information theory and multivariate analysis. According to the studies of perception, people normally avoid uncertainty so much that they will refuse to see, hear, smell, or feel what they believe should not be; they will insist on a fantasy as factual evidence. In terms of non-verbal thought, this means that we cannot directly know external events; that our senses and sensations and ideas give us, at most, a prognosis of their significance. What is known can never exactly correspond to the immediate occasion. At best their relationship can only be a similarity or analogy. The degree of this similarity may vary, but we can never know the inherent nature of objects and their relationships as such.

The fact that we can never know what we commonly consider as facts and truth is rather appalling. It is as if nature had set about to create a super hoax with humans, like donkeys chasing a "feed bag." But we are in that situation as long as we insist on believing that knowledge of the constitution of things as such, and their relationships, is the final goal.

It is only when we recognize that so-called facts and truths in themselves are not the ultimate goal, but have value in so far as they show us the ever becoming reality and contribute to our purposes, that we shall cease to be hoaxed.[4]

This observation explains some of the elusiveness inherent in action-based, non-verbal thinking. At the same time, it provides an entry to that thinking in terms of the prognosis or interpretation. If senses and sensations give only a prognosis of what is expected, the nature of non-verbal thought might be revealed within that expectation. Yet expectation is a mental construction that can typically be verbalized; and the search for typical sources can come away from complex psychological studies into the familiar world of prose. The search for principles has followed a detour, from words, to information theory, to uncertainty, to perception, to expectation, and back to words. The search has been qualified, however, as a search for non-verbal uncertainty, which is verbalized as expectation within written prose.

Furthermore, studies with perception show how this can be done; they show that abstractions identify successful perceptions, which experience shows may be repeated; and for this reason, abstractions are by nature without a point of view. Any abstraction must be given a point of view before it can use senses and sensations as a prognosis, and that point of view can be obtained through a known purpose. Thus purpose becomes critical to perception of abstract experience. Similarly, a sensation must achieve significance through purpose before that sensation can act as a guide for action. Purpose is critical to senses and sensations; it appears as the next step in the search for translating thoughts into prose. Two kinds of purpose are involved: (1) a personalizing purpose that gives abstractions a point of view; and (2) a purpose for action that selects among several sources of information for a guide. These two kinds of purpose, abstract and active, show where to look for and use uncertainty in organizing prose.

This can be demonstrated practically through three descriptions of the game of baseball. The first has no purpose and is said to have been incomprehensible to anyone who did not already know the game. The second shows the success achieved through giving the abstraction, *baseball*, a generalized purpose. The third, which personalizes purpose in terms of an individual player, shows how to achieve a description in terms of purposeful action.

Here is the description that expresses no purpose:

> Baseball is played with a bat and a ball on a level field at one end of which is a square, or "diamond," 90 feet on a side. One point of this square is home plate and the sides of the playing field extend at least 250 feet from the point of the square which is "home plate." The other three points of the 90-foot square are the three bases—first, second, and third in counterclockwise order. There are nine players on each team. One team is in the "field" while the other team is "at bat."
>
> The bat is made of wood not more than 42 inches long (usually not more than 36 inches) and not over 2-3/4 inches in diameter at the thickest part. The "home plate" is five-sided, 17 inches wide across the front, and 6-1/2 inches long on each of the two sides adjacent to the 17-inch front edge. From these two 6-1/2 inch sides two twelve-inch sides meet in a point at the back of the center of the plate. Each of the bases is 15 inches square.
>
> The "catcher" stands behind home plate. The "pitcher"...[5]

and so forth.

Here is the description that assigns a purpose to the abstraction, *baseball*:

> Baseball is a contest between two teams of nine players each, the winning of which is decided by the number of "runs" each team has made by the end of a legal game. A legal game of baseball usually consists of nine co-ordinate "innings" or nine turns "at bat" for each team. The team that is having one of its turns at bat is on the offensive; it is seeking to make "runs." Runs are made as follows...[6]

and so forth.

Here is the description that assigns a purpose to the actions of individual players, in this case, the batter:

> Sooner or later, every player on a baseball team must take his turn at bat. Standing beside home plate, a five-cornered plaque imbedded in the ground at his feet and wielding a 3-foot club called a "bat," the batter tries to hit a hard, 3-inch diameter baseball hurled by a pitcher standing about 60 feet away. If the batter swings and misses, a "strike" is called against him; if the ball fails to cross home plate at a level between his shoulders and knees, a "ball" is called against the pitcher. If the batter misses three times, he is "out"; if the pitcher misses four times, the batter gets to "walk" to his first "base." If the batter connects, he is allowed to touch as many bases as he can run over,

starting on his right, before the ball is picked up and put at one of the bases. There are three bases, 90 feet apart, at three corners of a square joined to home plate, which makes the fourth corner. Thus the batter usually tries to hit the baseball as hard as he can. If he hits it so far that he can run to touch all three bases and get back to home plate before the baseball is returned, that is called hitting a "home run," a feat much admired by baseball players.

If the batter connects and fails to reach first base before the baseball, he is out; if he reaches first base to find an opposing player holding the baseball on the second base, he has made a "single" and waits on first for the next player of his team to take the turn at bat.

While his team mates wait, the batter alone is pitted against all nine members of the opposing team. Eight of those players, including the pitcher, occupy places on and beyond the square of the bases, so as to be ready to quickly capture the flying baseball and get it to a plate before the running batter arrives there. The ninth player, called the "catcher" squats behind home plate to the rear of the batter, so as to catch strikes and balls thrown by the pitcher. If any one of the nine opposing players catches a hit ball before it touches the ground, the batter is out.

Each team is allowed a total of three outs, before it must...

and so forth.

These three excerpts show three different ways of saying the same thing. They put to the test most of the principles heretofore set forth in this book. Their message is as complex as most messages about professional activity, because baseball is as complex as most professional subjects. And the descriptions offer examples of translating transient action-based thoughts into prose because most of the thoughts expressed in baseball are expressed in short-lived actions. It can be useful to consider each of the excerpts separately for the kind of writing it represents, and to ask some questions, such as: Of what use is this kind of writing? What are its limitations? How does this writing fit the SPRI classes of thought?

The description that expresses no purpose. This type of writing is highly useful and common. It is found in handbooks and academic texts, where the reader-user is expected to have some knowledge of the subject and an intent to learn facts. Compositions of this sort can usually assemble, in the manner of a chart or table, the most data in the least amount of space. Moreover, this kind of writing is easiest to compose; the author can present the data as it comes to mind without too much attention to what comes before or after. To the extent that the contents of this message are original or unfamiliar to the reader, however, this type of composition is of little or no use. In spite of grammatically perfect sentences, the reader simply will not be able to grasp what the author is driving at without expression of some purpose, point of view, or problem. The data will not appear as information, nor will the concepts be recognizable. Consequently, this kind of writing should not be used any time an author wants to propose personal or unique ideas. There is no point of view, no purpose, no uncertainty, no information, and no concept; the form does not fit any part of SPRI, nor does it relate thought to prose.

The description that assigns a purpose to an abstraction. The form of this description presents an archetype of the resolution-information thought classes described in chapter 2. In the second description, the frame for a balanced SPRI composition might be completed by adding a few introductory paragraphs that describe the near-insane preoccupation that seems to dominate the United States at World Series time in the fall, followed by a question as to what the source of this mood is, and the answer that the source is "baseball." The composition would then enter directly into the sample paragraph. Such a composition would be an article of concept formation, in which the formed concept would be *baseball*. As it stands, however, the sample paragraph assumes that the reader brings along at least a knowledge of the word, *baseball*, and some curiosity about it. Accordingly, this type of writing corresponds to the kind of descriptions one might find in an encyclopedia. Also, it might be part of a booklet of procedural instructions, as well as some textbooks. But without a suitable introduction, this form could not be used to present an author's ideas.

The description that assigns individual purpose. This form of composition is sometimes called "narrative," because it is often used by novelists. Through assigning a purpose and locating the point of view with a sympathetic character, novelists can achieve dramatic moments by taking that character into crises. Also, this personalized point of view is used by popular news magazines to introduce a general subject. If for example, the United States Supreme Court is to try an important case, a news magazine might introduce an article on that subject by taking the personal point of view and purposes of one of the protagonists, and describing a sequence of intimate events leading up to the abstract problem that produced the court case. Thus this form of composition fits the situation class of thoughts described in Chapter 2.

The foregoing description could also be adapted for the situation for an article on baseball umpires. Describing the action from the batter's point of view serves to intensify the sense of the abstract problem occurring when the ball and a batter arrive at first base at the same time, or when the bases are loaded with two strikes and three balls, and the next pitch is allowed to pass over a corner of the plate. Who decides whether the batter is safe or out? Accordingly, this form of composition translates specific action-based thoughts into prose; and it is the most effective way to introduce unfamiliar thoughts such as might be associated with a discovery.

However, individual purposes and their uncertainties are not suited to serve for an abstract problem and its resolution; and those thought classes must be added, usually with a change in point of view, in order for this form to introduce an SPRI frame article. Also, this form requires more words to present the same information as the other two forms. Finally, this form is difficult, because the writer must constantly judge whether a bit of information is necessary or distracting to the reader. For example, the second sentence of the excerpt may have read: "Standing beside home plate, the batter tries...," and it may have gone into a description of the pitcher's mound with the subsequent sentence. Thus the professional who would write must come to grips with the compositional form of individual purpose and its associated creation and resolutions of uncertainties through successive words and word groups.

Because readers try to avoid noticing uncertainty, they are tolerant of any specific choice of form. However, they become bored and impatient if the sense of a continuing release of information is lost. For this reason, interesting prose requires its author to be alert to creating more uncertainty with the same words that resolve a previous uncertainty, while at the same time directing the string of thoughts toward an objective. This task is not so difficult as it may seem, once it is articulated; and it is made easier through an understanding of the usual forms of uncertainty. These will be discussed in the following sections.

HOW TO FIND QUESTIONS IN CONCEPTS

Consider again a passage quoted under "Feedback" in Chapter 2, plus a few sentences offered later on in the same text.[7]

Action-produced stimulation is obtained, not imposed—that is, obtained by the individual, not imposed on him. It is intrinsic to the flow of activity, not extrinsic to it; dependent on it, not independent of it.... It is not simply forced on the individual. Animals and men can select or enhance the stimuli they receive from the world, or even exclude certain kinds, by orienting and adjusting their sense organs.

These statements are so close to most persons' sense of reality that they are accepted as intuitively obvious. Yet the application of these statements to prose composition opens up some remarkable possibilities. It is in the nature of readers to bend their attention to the directions indicated in the prose. As an author directs their attention, the readers orient and adjust their senses to select and enhance remembered sense impressions to go with the verbal stimuli that the author puts before them. When the focus of the directed attention is a concept, the readers automatically adjust their senses to receive information about that concept. That is, they willingly enter into uncertainty in the good faith that the uncertainty will promptly be resolved. Here are some examples.

First, the perception of a geological phenomenon:

For over three weeks our army from the Sudan had been encamped at the edge of the plain from which I write this dispatch, with what seemed an insurmountable obstacle before them—the buttress of the Eritrean escarpment. It is a cliff of solid rock, thousands of feet high, and in parts sheer precipice, crowned with a row of peaks like stone arrow-heads. These form a ridge behind which lies Keren. The only road to Keren from the plain used to slant across the cliff face, but the Italians, experts in demolition, blasted it away some time ago.

A screen of skirmishers began to climb the cliff by moonlight... We moved cautiously up the last passable stretch of road that mounted from the plain to the base of the cliff.[8]

Next, a description of a book:

There are times when bringing together known information can result in a synergistic association that affords unprecedented effectiveness for that information. The authors have achieved such a synergism with this book.

Profitability calculations, market research, chemical engineering cost estimating, and shortcut process design methods, which are all discussed here, are well-known skills. However anyone who has ever faced a feasibility study for a refining, a petrochemical, or a chemical plant will have discovered that finding reliable answers is something following a will-o'-the wisp. Profitability depends on revenues, operating costs, and investment, which in turn depend on market conditions, manufacturing efficiencies, and cost...[9]

Next, a description of patents:

Much that has been written about patents can be traced to two fundamental qualities. They are (1) exclusive, rather than inclusive; and (2) represent a legal monopoly granted in exchange for public disclosure (in the specification of the patent, preceding the claims) of useful, novel information. The exclusive nature of patents is defined by some five inherent rights of the patent owner, while the limits of the monopoly are defined by some three proper uses.[10]

Next a description of the origins of the atmosphere:

Modern astronomers tell us that the quantity of fixed nitrogen in the world has been decreasing for a long time. They say that the primeval atmosphere was composed principally of hydrogen, ammonia, water vapor, and methane.

There was little free nitrogen, and the atmospheric oxygen on which life now depends was tied up in metal oxides in the rocks and in the water. Gradually the free hydrogen, which is too light to be held in the atmosphere of a planet of the size of the Earth, was lost to space, while ammonia dissociated into nitrogen and hydrogen.

The oxygen of our present atmosphere has been produced by plant life, which is believed to have descended from initial life forms that were born in the less harsh, reducing atmospheres of those primeval times. After chlorophyl appeared in plants, ...[11]

and so forth.

Although the things described in these four examples range from the Eritrean escarpment to a book on economic analysis, to patents, to the origin of the atmosphere, the same method was used to introduce all of them. A declamatory sentence focused attention on some feature of the concept to be described. The Eritrean escarpment (concept) was an insurmountable obstacle (feature); the book (concept) was synergistic (feature); patents (concept) had two fundamental qualities (feature); and the free (non-fixed) nitrogen of the atmosphere (concept) had been a long time getting there (feature). This association of concept plus feature of that concept introduced an acceptable uncertainty to the reader. It shows how an author can add facts with a three-step method: (1) choose a concept to signify the collected facts; (2) choose a feature of that concept involving some remarkable generality; and (3) make a statement relating the concept and the feature. This statement sets up uncertainties for information that can usually be set down in one to three paragraphs. The paragraphs can be part of either the situation class or the information class of an SPRI frame article.

In the following example, the authors are discussing the peculiarities of English. Among those peculiarities is the relative suitability of English for handling logic. Their concept is "English," which signifies all of the language; the chosen feature is "illogical"; and their introductory statement reads:

As for the view that English is illogical: ...

The information follows right after the colon:

it certainly differs greatly in character from French, Italian, Spanish and German, which are claimed to be logical languages. These are all able codifications of as much racial experience as can be translated into speech: Theoretically, each separate object, process or quality is given a registered label and ever afterwards recognized by label rather than by individual quality. Logical languages are therefore also rhetorical languages, rhetoric being the emotionally persuasive use of labels, with little concern for the things to which they are tied. English has always tended to be a language of "conceits": that is, except for the purely syntactical parts of speech, which are in general colorless, the vocabulary is not fully dissociated from the imagery out of which it has developed—words are pictures, rather than hieroglyphs....

"Fixed" English, which may be dated from Dr. Johnson's *Dictionary*, completed in 1755, fulfills the need of a safer, less ambiguous language arranged on the same system and dedicated to the same rules as French—a language of agreed preconceptions. "Fixed" English makes possible a French-English, English-French, or a German-English, English-German dictionary. Each foreign label has its English counterpart: "Glory" is matched (not very satisfactorily) with "*la gloire*" and "*der Ruhm*"; "*le matelot*" and "*der Matrose*" with "sailor." "Fixed" English compares well enough with other languages, but is often more mechanically, and...[12]

and so forth.

This example again shows how a concept may carry a meaning of signification, relating thoughts with their own internal structure to a verbal statement which has its separate structure. The example thus affords another proof of the analogy to mathematical structures made in the introduction to this chapter.

When a concept is used to signify a meaning in this way, the uncertainties it introduces are different from the concept's characteristic problems described in Chapter 2. Whereas the uncertainties are satisfied by facts, the characteristic problems are resolved only with another concept. The difference is signalled by the manner of introduction, signification being related to some feature and another concept being related to a specific question.

However, concepts are but one source of the uncertainties with which a composition is tied together. Other sources occur in familiar rules for writing, which need to be turned inside out for their uncertainties. For example, uncertainties can be found in Rudyard Kipling's well-known stanza:

> I keep six honest serving men
>   (They taught me all I knew);
> Their names are What and Why and
>   When
> And How and Where and Who.[13]

KIPLING'S Ws REVISITED

Rudyard Kipling's Ws are indirectly responsible for the SPRI classification of thought. A new assistant editor at *Chemical Week* had been trained technically but had no training in journalism. Somewhere, he had learned the rule, common among newspaper writers, that the proper way to begin an article was to tell the readers as soon as possible the answers to *what, why, when, where,* and *who*. He did this, with the result that, after days of research and interviews, he would write two or three carefully worded paragraphs and not know how to continue. An article outline proposed to break this writing block became the frame into which thoughts were substituted for classification.

That assistant editor's problem is widespread among people making a first effort to write for publication. They need a way to get started; they need some guidelines as to what they ought to say and how they ought to say it; and they are usually inhibited by half-learned, negative rules of "correct" grammar, such as not to split an infinitive and not to end a sentence with an adverb. Without the SPRI frame for article composition, they are unaware that their writing should build to a problem and its resolution, and that this problem/resolution should be a specific subject of interest to their readers. Without the knowledge of uncertainty, of purpose, and of point of view, they are unaware that these must be present for their prose to be comprehensible to anyone who is not already familiar with the subject. Consequently they set out to tell *what, where, why, when,* and *who* without assuming any purpose for the composition other than grammatically perfect English. The result is usually analogous to the purposeless description of the game of baseball given earlier.

Even so, the traditional "Ws" type of writing holds for American newspapers a place that tends to keep its dogmatic principles firmly entrenched in the minds of teachers of journalism. This dates from the U.S. Civil War, when uncertain telegraph service was likely to interrupt at any point the dispatches sent back to newspaper offices from reporters at the battle zones. These reporters and their editors evolved the so-called triangular style: The first paragraph gave the five Ws; then the next few paragraphs took those Ws and elaborated on them a bit; and then the subsequent paragraphs repeated the process, taking the previous descriptions and elaborating on them until the reporter's information or imagination were exhausted. The quality of the writing was usually judged by how florid it was made through active verbs and dramatic adjectives.

This triangular style persists in many newspapers today, under a similar assumption that the article may be interrupted at any time. Instead of from the telegraph service, however, today's interruptions come from the newspaper's layout and bored readers. The article can be introduced with a few paragraphs beneath a headline, and then interrupted to be continued on a remote page. If the reader has already formed an interest in the subject, he or she may seek out that page and continue reading. More often, the article is abandoned at the point where it is to be continued.

This has a great practical use for newspaper publishers, who gain an important part of their income from advertising. There are restrictions about the ratio of editorial copy to advertisements, so that more ads need more columns of writing and vice versa. The ratio is easily maintained by publishing a first page with the beginnings of many triangular style articles and little or no advertising. Those articles can then be cut off or extended in the back pages for as long as there are ads to support them. An example of the sort of lead newspapers might use to tease their readers into reading around the ads in the back pages is the following:

> Fifteen unkempt Greek guerrillas who helped shell Salonika six weeks ago were executed by firing squads today, as a clammy dawn routed the shadows from a sixth-century citadel frowning down on the death scene.

Obviously, this paragraph tells *who, why, what, when,* and *where*. The drama of the description keeps one reading to its end; and there is a fair chance that a reader might turn the page to read on. If so, it is almost certain that the reader will be seeking to learn more about *who* (the fifteen guerrillas), *why* (the shelling at Salonika), and *where* (the sixth-century citadel). The manner of presenting *when* (six weeks ago and today at dawn) and *what* (executed by firing squads) carries a finality that inhibits further reading. This particular article is thus prepared to be supported on three simultaneous discussions, like a three-legged stool.

Assume for comparison that the purpose of the paragraph was to stimulate interest in the relative strengths of the Greek government and the guerrilla movement, which the reporter might have discovered through on-the-spot investigation. The lead might go:

> Only six weeks after Salonika was shelled, fifteen of the Greek guerrillas were executed today.

This lead skips the question of *where* entirely, and by using the modified *only* concentrates uncertainty on the six weeks. If the subject were retribution, the same information could be arranged to read:

> Six weeks after Greek guerrillas shelled Salonika, fifteen of the guerrillas were executed today.

Here, *fifteen* leads to uncertainty as to the total number of guerrillas involved. The information is essentially the same as in the original lead, but the reader now expects to find a discussion of the capture of the guerrillas, with perhaps an analysis of the guerrilla movement and its repression by the government.

In the same way as with this example, most five-W leads can be adapted for introducing an article that uses the SPRI frame to present a rational conclusion. The writer needs only to determine which of the standard questions to stress. Instead of the newspaper reporter's five, however, one can choose from Kipling's six: *who, what, where, when, why,* and *how.* If, for example, execution by firing squad (how) signified something about the Greek government, the same information as the original lead could be presented as:

Firing squads today executed fifteen of the Greek guerrillas who shelled Salonika six weeks ago.

Taken together, these various arrangements of the same information suggest that Kipling's six questions represent the dimensions of uncertainty in the real world. Most important, the newspaper reporter's rule of five Ws should be understood as a source of bad writing. Readers do not normally approach a new article with questions in mind, so that carefully answering a dogmatic list of five questions succeeds only in providing the kind of statements that information theorists call "noise." Instead of thoughtlessly writing down a checklist of answers to unasked questions, an author should decide on the type of uncertainty to be created, and then build on that. Here, for example, are some paragraphs built around *when*:

Many years ago, I would go to bed early. Sometimes, as I snuffed my candle, my eyes closed so fast I didn't have time to say to myself, "I'm going to sleep." And half an hour later, the thought that it was time to go to sleep would wake me; I wanted to lay aside the book I imagined in my hands and to blow out the light; it seemed that I myself was the thing written about: a church, a quartet, the rivalry between Francis I and Charles V. This belief would last during several wakeful seconds; it didn't seem unreasonable, but weighed like scales on my eyes and kept them from realizing that the candle wasn't lit.

This is my translation of the beginning of "Combray," the first part of Marcel Proust's novel, *In Search of Times Past*. The writing is a phenomenally good example of description that assigns an individual purpose. The perspective is so close to the author that the reader is taken even behind the author's eyelids. Furthermore, the methods displayed in this first paragraph are repeated throughout the novel, until the reader is made to feel one with the protagonist. At the end of the passage, the same method is turned into its mirror image to create the opposite effect. Starting from an intimate point of view, Proust gently but deliberately carries the readers outside again and leaves them there.

Surely, I was wide awake now: my body had come together a last time and the good angel of stability had stopped everything around me, had layed me under my covers, in my room, and had approximately placed in the shadows my bedside table, my fireplace, my desk, the window overlooking the street, and the two doors.

Now let's see what Kipling's six serving men can tell us about these passages.

The first passage is dominated by *when*, the last by *where*. In the first passage, the sense of *when* is made more and more precise, from a span of years to "early," to a snuff of a candle, to half an hour, to seconds. In the last passage, the sense of *where* is expanded from the boy's body to his bed, to his room, to the furniture near then far, to the window, the doors, and the street outside. In the first passage the sense of other uncertainties (*what, why, how*, etc.) surrounding an increasingly specific time are allowed to build for two sentences plus the phrase "and half an hour later." At that point, the tension of built uncertainty is sufficient to endure two long compound sentences joined by three semicolons and a colon, all around *what*.

This rhythmic build-up and dissipation of uncertainty is used to create extremely vivid, specifically personal points of view throughout the novel. And in the closing passage, when Proust wants to release readers from his narrow point of view, with the mirror image of the method, the sense of *where* is defined surely and then reinforced redundantly with a recitation of objects ever further away.

Although writing about the professions can hardly be expected to exhibit Marcel Proust's charm, it can imitate his use of the uncertainties in Kipling's Ws to sustain interest in dry passages of how-to instructions. People generally want to communicate. Those who would communicate by writing must respect the formal rules of written language. In addition, those who would write about a profession must also respect the formal disciplines of thought of that profession. Thus a professional who writes must combine two formal disciplines, that of writing and that of the profession; words that stand for ideas must be combined so as to suit both their syntactical and their thoughtful relations at the same time; and ideas whose words can not be joined in satisfactory syntax can only be related in some substitute fashion, such as analogy. In this situation, words whose signified thoughts do have many possible applications become critically useful; and six such words are *who, when, what, where, why,* and *how*.

In the above paragraph, attention was focused on *who*, which was narrowed from people in general to a professional who writes, when *what* was introduced as the combined restriction of thought and language, and extended into two long sentences joined by semicolons. Only two out of the six possible *W*s were involved in the statements, yet the reader does not suffer any uneasiness about lack of information concerning *when, where, why,* and *how.* It becomes obvious that the rule of five *W*s does not enumerate what needs to be said so much as it offers subjects for discussion to writers who do not know what else to say. On the other hand, a review of Proust's introduction to "Combray" shows that the increasingly specific description of *when* in the first two and one half sentences does build up some sort of expectation about descriptions to follow. Similarly, the increasingly specific description of *who* in the preceding paragraph prepares the reader for a long sentence about *what* in terms of words and ideas. It becomes apparent that the structure of a paragraph can introduce an ambiguity about the thought. If that ambiguity is ignored, it becomes distracting to the reader; if it is used to enhance the thought, it makes the writing interesting. The question is *how*; ambiguity has become the key.

AMBIGUITY THAT HINDERS HELPS

Here again is the passage by Adelbert Ames, Jr.:

The fact that we can never know what we commonly consider as facts and truth is rather appalling. It is as if nature had set about to create a super hoax with humans, like donkeys chasing a "feed bag." But we are in that situation as long as we insist on believing that knowledge of the constitution of things as such, and their relationships, is the final goal.

It is only when we recognize that so-called facts and truths in themselves are not the ultimate goal, but have value in so far as they show us the ever becoming reality and contribute to our purposes, that we shall cease to be hoaxed.[14]

These observations, which are based on empirical tests in perception, were used earlier to show the elusiveness of action-based, non-verbal thinking. Subsequently, one may have come to the opinion that the dynamic, constantly changing nature of facts and thoughts was changed by writing things down and fixing them on paper with words. However, this is not the case. Reading and writing are sequential activities, in which the understanding of the present word is conditioned by what went before, as that understanding conditions our understanding of words to come. Because we approach reading and writing with a purpose, our understanding and our expression are affected not only by the words just passed but also by the present purpose. Rereading a passage is thus analogous to shopping along the aisle of a supermarket; the produce on the shelves remains the same, but the things selected vary both with the purposes of the individual shopper and the selections just made. Within this on-going process, an uncertainty that is intimately involved with purpose causes one to react positively to things that suit the purpose, while a confusing array of choices that do not suit the purpose are passed over. To the extent that the things passed over intrude on one's consciousness they have been described by information theorists as "noise"; and it is the noise of aggressively displayed unwanted items in a supermarket that makes supermarket shopping unpleasant to many people.

One can say that ambiguity is the same as uncertainty, and that the greater the ambiguity the greater the uncertainty and the information that resolves it. The difference between the two can be demonstrated by returning to the original experiments that introduced information theory. English sentences were read aloud, letter by letter, to a co-experimenter, and he or she guessed each subsequent letter before it was read. Since there are twenty-six letters in the English alphabet, it is theoretically possible, by continually dividing the twenty-six letters into two groups of thirteen, six and seven, three and four, and two, to always arrive at the correct letter within five guesses, so that the maximum information corresponding to any letter is five bits. However, there are many spelling conventions that make so many guesses unnecessary. If two subsequent letters are t and h, for example, there is a high probability that the next letter will be e; and it is in this way that the information theorists decided that English is 50 percent redundant. But the information theorists make an assumption that can not be extended to reading and writing in general. What about misspellings and bad grammar? To the extent that words are misspelled or that the grammar is incorrect, the uncertainty is thrown right back to the maximum of five bits; and using the word *ambiguity* to describe that form of uncertainty, it is possible to make several observations directly from experience.

Ambiguity comes out of things past, rather than from out of a purpose and the future. To the extent that it disrupts the orderly relation between purpose and uncertainty, ambiguity is disturbing, confusing, and undesirable. Yet by creating uncertainty and thus a potential for information, it is possible that ambiguity can make writing more interesting. It becomes apparent that ambiguity hinders so long as it comes from a disturbance of the formal structures; and it helps when it relates to the non-formal pattern of events in the real world. Specifically, ambiguity helps when it results from a deliberate disregard of the newspaper reporter's five Ws. The previous passage from "Combray" demonstrated this; short stories demonstrate it so consistently that creating ambiguity might be considered a short story technique. Here are some examples.

From the beginning of "The Three Strangers," by Thomas Hardy:

> Among the few features of agricultural England which retain an appearance but little modified by the lapse of centuries may be reckoned the high, grassy

and furzy downs, coombs, or ewe-leases, as they are indifferently called, that fill a large area of certain counties in the south and southwest. If any mark of human occupation is met with hereon, it usually takes the form of the solitary cottage of some sheperd.

Fifty years ago such a lonely cottage stood...[15]

and so forth. From this beginning of *where* the story carefully builds up uncertainty about the identities of the three strangers (the thief, his executioner, and the thief's brother), or *who*, by elaborating on *what*, *where*, *how*, and *why* as they related to the sheperd's cottage.

From the beginning of "The Killers," by Ernest Hemingway:

The door of Henry's lunchroom opened and two men came in. They sat down at the counter.
"What's yours?" George asked them.
"I don't know," one of the men said. "What do you want to eat, Al?"
"I don't know," said Al. "I don't know what I want to eat."
Outside it was getting dark. The street-light came on outside the window. The two men at the counter read the menu. From the other end of the counter...[16]

and so forth. The two men proceed to show themselves bullies, but it is not before the climax two-thirds of the way through that Hemingway shows that they are killers come to kill Ole Anderson, who normally eats at the lunch counter at 6:00 o'clock. Here we have an elaboration of *who* while tension builds about the untold answers to the other Ws.

Unlike short stories, an article for a professional journal will have facts to communicate. Rather than build uncertainty in terms of the Ws, therefore, the article can often stimulate interest by describing the problems that led to the revelation of the facts. As science and technology become more complex, the same sets of facts come to mean different things in different situations; and it becomes increasingly necessary to avoid misunderstanding by packaging the facts in an introduction that emphasizes a specific attitude toward those facts. This introduction will rarely address the main thesis directly; and it will often create uncertainty by manipulating the Ws. Some examples follow.

A conversation with Aldous Huxley not infrequently put one at the receiving end of an unforgettable monologue. About a year before his lamented death he was discoursing on a favorite topic: Man's unnatural treatment of nature and its sad results. To illustrate his point he told how, during the previous summer, he had returned to a little valley in England where he had spent many happy months as a child. Once it had been composed of delightful grassy glades; now it was becoming overgrown with unsightly brush because the rabbits that formerly kept such growth under control had largely succumbed to a disease, myxomatosis, that was deliberately introduced by the local farmers to reduce the rabbits' destruction of crops. Being something of a Philistine, I could be silent no longer, even in the interests of great rhetoric. I interrupted to point out that the rabbit itself had been brought as a domestic animal to England in 1176, presumably to improve the protein diet of the peasantry.[17]

White goes on to explain that, whereas all forms of life modify their environment, humans have learned to go beyond passive modification to impersonally exploit nature, and that anthropocentric religions encourage the exploitative attitude. His introduction thus serves as an analogy for the misunderstandings that surround this thesis.

1:15 A.M.: Dense cloud cover masks the moon. The cool wind is light but steady from the south, and I can barely hear the high-pitched squeals of grasshopper mice in the distance. From the corner of my eye, I glimpse a bannertail kangaroo rat chasing an intruder from the territory near its mound. And just thirty feet to my left is a Mojave rattlesnake, probably the same one I saw last night, hoping one of those rodents will pass its way. In the light cast by my miner's headlamp, I can see a column of ants rapidly crossing the desert floor. They are members of *Neivamyrmex nigrescens*, a species of army ant, and they are intent on raiding and robbing...[18]

and so forth. This introduction presents a detailed description, in terms of *where*, *when*, and *why*, which serves to set the situation for subsequent abstract discussions of how the different ants muster recruits, attack, retreat, counterattack, wage chemical warfare, and even display a site occupation strategy similar to that proposed for the MX missiles.

For several years, the research team of a large chemical manufacturing group had worked on a project which had grown out of a simple idea. Their object had been to develop a series of agricultural fertilizers which would contain the principal plant foods and important trace substances intermixed with differing proportions of several calcium salts which would break down at distinct time rates, releasing the nutrients over a period of several years. Just which chemicals would be present and in what proportions would be arranged to suit the crop, the soil where it would be grown, and the climate. Their work had been associated with tests at a number of agricultural research stations in home and overseas territories and had been shown to be brilliantly successful.
In anticipation of this...[19]

and so forth. This is the beginning of a well-written book on civil engineering for other engineering specialists and managers who need to understand civil engineering work although not actually doing it.

The book clearly explains the roster of civil engineering functions and designs by assigning them the purposes of building and maintaining an ammonia plant.

The foregoing passages should demonstrate that an attempt to address the central thesis of an article at the beginning is not only unnecessary but is usually detrimental. On the other hand, it is always necessary to be clear about who is addressing whom on the subject of what—about which of several previous notions are being discussed, and about how the sense of the present sentence suits that of sentences just passed. Generally, these things are handled through mechanisms within English grammar, as will be described in the next chapter. For now, it is time to review and relate the several points brought up in this chapter through feedback.

FEEDBACK FOR CHAPTER 3

The notions set forth in this chapter have several times come close to notions carried in more conventional treatises on writing, sometimes by way of reinforcement and sometimes in conflict. Readers may have found some things that correspond to previous ideas, and may have consequently been tempted to fit pieces of this text into some other pattern. That may be good, or not so good; whichever, some perspective is useful at this point.

I know of but one exception[20] to the generalization that books on writing assume (1) that clear prose indicates superior intelligence or cultural background and (2) that the essence of graceful, interesting, and attractive writing is found in metaphors and analogies. This book assumes, by comparison, (1) that clear prose indicates nothing more than a skill at writing, either natural or acquired, and (2) that since signifying words are themselves metonyms for parts of the real world, and since verbal thoughts are analogies for the ephemeral perceptions of the real world, the emphasis on metaphors and analogies is simplistic. You can learn, consciously, to write clearly and gracefully; and part of that learning is a comprehension of analogies and metaphors that allows you to package them in simple, obvious statements that appeal to readers.

Linguists have long recognized an aspect of language that they term *immediate constituents*, and generally group into various levels. This book recognizes a similar grouping. There is the classification and organization of thought, presented in Chapter 2; there is the use of formal English, which will be presented in Chapter 4; and in between those two, there is the translation of thought into language, which is the subject of this chapter. Problems uncovered through the organization of thought are discussed in this chapter; problems uncovered through the translation of thought into language are discussed in Chapter 4.

This chapter is based on the following theses: All humans have a vast repertoire of thoughts, which are used to cope with the real world. These thoughts are ephemeral, conditioned by desire and purpose, and only partly realized by perceptions, actions, and words. Words can represent thoughts by acting either as images or fixed hieroglyphs. Words as images are flexible, corresponding to free English necessary for representing the real technical world. Words as hieroglyphs are rigid, corresponding to fixed English useful for logic and for organizing ideas with mathematical precision. Words as images are compatible with the notions of trial and error, design choices, and feedback expressed in Chapter 2. Just as desire and purpose condition perception in the real world, so they condition the understanding of words. Moreover, words can be used to express desire and purpose, such that they lead to uncertainty, which is necessary for verbal comprehension. The scope of uncertainty is contained in the ideas of *why*, *what*, *when*, and *where* and *how* and *who*; and because we already know this intuitively, non-verbalized dimensions of uncertainty can be brought out as ambiguity through verbal descriptions that detail one of the dimensions, such as *when* or *what*.

Chapter 3 has attempted to demonstrate these theses through descriptions and examples. While the theses do support each other, there has been no attempt to make any part of the exposition logical or to rely on a consistent definition of terms. The chapter began by relying on experience and common sense to show that humans do think without words, in order to help readers be alert to their own non-verbal thoughts.

With the existence of non-verbal thoughts realized, the problem for the writer becomes that of attaching words to those thoughts. This was described as an extremely difficult problem. Remembering the concepts of Chapters 1 and 2, the act of verbalizing thought can be seen as an act of expanding consciousness. As long as the words are used freely and flexibly as images, they can serve to convert non-verbalized thoughts from being rigid, labile, diffuse, inarticulate, and syncretic into thoughts that are flexible, stable, discrete, articulated, and definite. In order to accomplish this feat, we took an arbitrary analogy from information theory. Through this analogy, the formal structures of English were likened to the formal structure of mathematical multivariate analysis, so that an internal thought structure could be related to an external prose structure through the significance of words as symbols for concepts. This analogy led to a search for uncertainty, existing as the variables possible in a thought, as the key to clear and interesting writing. Then this notion of uncertainty was tested against common experience.

The first test was made through references to experiments with perception; and it showed that the acts of perceiving are as unreliable and ephemeral as the thoughts we would put words to. However, interpretations of perception made by Adelbert Ames, Jr., identified prognosis or expectation as crucial. Assuming by analogy that verbalized prognoses might be used for putting words to thought, we extended Adelbert Ames's notion to expressions of purpose, either general or specific. This use of purpose was then tested against empirical experiments with descriptions of the game of baseball made by C. C. Fries. He compared two descriptions, one purposeless and incomprehensible, and another with an abstract purpose and understandable. To those we added a third description with an individualized purpose. The three types of description—purposeless, abstract purpose, and individualized purpose—thus identified could be illustrated by various types of useful prose.

With a hold on unwritten thoughts thus obtained through experience with perception, our attention then turned to concepts, in order to see what perception and the use of purpose might yield. We found that authors and readers alike will allow their attention to be directed by the prose, and will allow a purpose to be indicated by the prose. Practically, this affords a three-step method for introducing facts so that they will be both interesting and understandable, as follows: (1) choose a concept that can signify the collected facts; (2) choose a feature of that concept involving some remarkable generality; and (3) make a statement relating concept and feature. Once this method is articulated, it can be seen as a source of uncertainty useful for paragraphs of facts presented in simple statements.

Since practical experience with perception had been so helpful in the search for useful uncertainties, it seemed that knowledge based on common experience might be searched for other useful forms of uncertainty. That search yielded Rudyard Kipling's six "serving men": *what, why, when, how, where,* and *who*. Various texts on writing discuss those questions. Unfortunately the tendency is to answer them as soon as possible. However, Kipling's suggestion that they are more complex ("They taught me all I knew"), plus recognizing the importance of uncertainty led us to test these six questions against some widely acknowledged prose passages. As a result, we saw that the questions *what, why, when, how, where,* and *who* appear to be known intuitively by everyone, as dimensions of uncertainty analogous to the dimensions of the physical world. Much interesting prose can be seen as the controlled build-up and dissipation of uncertainty through withholding and revealing the answers to those six questions.

Finally, the principles for writing stand only half-emerged from intuition. If they are to be joined to those of Chapter 2, these principles must be made part of habits and conditioning, so that they can make their appearance without conscious effort whenever composition has need of them. That calls for training and exercises.

EXERCISES

There is a useful analogy between writing and working in the woods. Our woods resembles much of New England in that it consists of pole-like trees 4–7 inches in diameter and 60–80 feet tall. These trees are much too close together; and about three-quarters of them are doomed to succumb and die in the competitive struggle among trees for available sunlight. Good forestry, at this point, consists of going through the woods, identifying those trees that are doomed, and harvesting most of them for firewood. In this way, the doomed trees are used, while the remaining trees are freed of competition to become stronger and faster growing.

However, harvesting pole trees 60–80 feet tall is not all that simple. These trees are clustered densely over acres of woodland, so that a falling tree can damage others or get caught in the branches of others and lead to some sort of accident. Also, since it is necessary to drag the felled trees out of the woods, it is possible to save much work by felling a tree in the direction it is to be taken out. These things, plus the patterns of growth, cause careful felling to be a mesh of complex decisions, which seem to be best made in groups of up to a dozen trees. Thus it is my practice to spend a few minutes planning: first, this into that opening, then this on top of the first, and then these two right down there, and so on.

A second problem—the one that suggests the analogy to writing—involves skill with a chain saw. Trees are felled in a given direction by cutting a "hinge" with an opposing notch in a tree's base. Considering that the hinge is less than 7 inches long, while the tree may be 70 feet tall, it is apparent that a fractional error in the notch can cause the top of the tree to come down several feet from the intended spot; and in a crowded woods those several feet can spell the difference between success and disaster. Because of this problem, my early group-felling projections were often more theoretical than factual. Over the years, however, practice with hundreds of trees has brought me to the point where I can say to myself, "This one there," and have it go there.

And that is exactly how it is with writing. If you choose the type of writing that places the words of your thoughts right next to previously verbalized thoughts, your mental attitude will be very close to mine in the woods. Harkening back to SPRI and the rise and fall of uncertainty, you will say of your thoughts, "I want this one here, that one there..." and so forth. Then you take a pencil or typewriter and set out to put them there. But just as it takes skill to fell a tree exactly in the designated direction, so it takes enormous skill to make words lay out a thought just as you want it. More times than not, your sentences, like the trees, will fall askew, and they will get into such a tangle that it becomes necessary to abandon the original plan just to sort out the tangle.

Patience! You must persist. If you don't, you will become a victim of your occupation. Up in the Northeast, that kind of impatient woodsman is distinguished by seven or eight out of ten fingers, about half a quota of teeth, a squint, and a limp. Although the hazards of failure at writing are not so evident, they are there nevertheless. On the other hand, if you do keep trying—keep saying and trying, "This one exactly right there, and that one there," the time will come when your words do obey. The satisfaction that comes with that experience is enormous—something beyond hope for those who search for thoughts in words they've already put to paper.

And of course that brings us to exercises. Theoretically, there should be hundreds of them. Practically, you should find these enough, because you will want to experiment with thoughts closer to your own interests. Do not delay, however. Develop the habit of rewriting every interesting document to come your way—now. You will not only hasten the acquisition of your own skills, you will learn more from and about those documents.

Considering the range of professions for which this book is intended, there seemed at first no possible subject that would suit most of the users, until—fortuituously—a marvelous book suggested itself: *Mastering the Art of French Cooking* by Simone Beck, Louisette Bertholle, and Julia Child. In this book, important recipes are accompanied by all the facts for an SPRI composition, so that it is only necessary to reorganize those facts to make a short SPRI essay for the recipe. Once you've done that for some recipes, you may want to compare your essays to other cookbooks. The experience may make you feel like writing your own cookbook. If it does, turn that feeling to your own profession, where you will find similar opportunities.

Presented below are the bare facts associated with each of half a dozen recipes including use, procedure, and proportions. You may want to supplement these facts with reference to an available cookbook. Once you feel you have the necessary information, you should compose a brief SPRI essay about the recipe. This essay should include...

for situation: a general description of the food that results from the recipe, including how it is used *for problem*: a discussion of the things that are most likely to cause this recipe to fail

for resolution: a discussion of the preparation step that overcomes the problem

for information: a discussion of how the critical step of the resolution is incorporated into the overall recipe; a recitation of the proportions of ingredients

You will find the author's attempts at essays for the selected recipes presented at the end of this book, under the heading, *Exercises: Examples*.

White Sauce

Description: A white or pale sauce thickened with flour.

Uses: This basic sauce stands at the head of a system of sauce making, in which the variants result from either enrichment with cream, butter or egg yolks, or from seasoning with cheese, tomatoes, wine and herbs, curry, or onions.

Problem: Flour can give a raw pasty taste to its medium.

Key Step: The flour is cooked in melted butter, so as to form a *roux*. This must be done at exactly the right temperature, with constant stirring for about two minutes, until the butter and flour froth together. Heating should then be stopped promptly.

Proportions: 2 volumes of butter to 3 volumes of flour. Each cup of added liquid requires a volume of flour, depending on the desired thickness, as follows:

for thin soup—	1 tablespoon
general purpose sauce—	1-1/2 tablespoon
thick sauce—	2 tablespoons
base for soufflé—	3 tablespoons

Brown Sauce

Description: A golden or brown sauce of bouillon or brown stock thickened with flour, frequently known as "gravy" in the U.S.

Uses: This basic sauce is the precursor of a range of sauces derived from cooking juices of meat, game or fowl.

Problem: The flour used to thicken these sauces can lend an unpleasant appearance and give a taste to the sauce.

Key Step: The flour must be cooked in the shortening until golden, and then simmered for 2 hours in the sauce.

Proportions: Each cup of finished sauce requires 1 tablespoon of flour, and 1-1/2 cups of stock or bouillon. Each tablespoon of flour requires 1-1/2 tablespoons of shortening. The shortening, which can be heated to a higher temperature than raw butter, may be clarified butter, rendered pork fat, or cooking oil.

Hollandaise Sauce

Description: A light, rich, thickly yellow cream sauce the color of butter and tasting of all its ingredients, egg yolks, butter and lemon juice.

Uses: This most elegant of sauces is always served warm, but not hot, over asparagus, poached eggs, boiled or poached fish, as a side dish for lobster and broiled fish, with soufflés, etc. Its derivative, bearnaise sauce, in which herb vinegar replaces the lemon juice, is served as a side dish with game and meat.

Problem: It is difficult to force egg yolks to emulsify butter.

Key Step: Before whipping in melted butter, the beaten mixture of egg yolks and seasoning is half cooked over simmering water by stirring it with a lump of butter until creamy.

Proportions: For about 1 cup of sauce: 12 tablespoons of butter, 1 tablespoon of lemon juice, 1 tablespoon of cold water, salt, 3 large egg yolks.

Mayonnaise

Description: A thick, medium-weight emulsion of oil in egg yolks.

Uses: Served at room temperature, either from a side dish or as a blanket over cold dishes, to add flavor and creamy texture.

Problem: Egg yolks can only emulsify a limited amount of oil and under only limited conditions.

Key Step: Beat salt and vinegar into the egg yolks in a warmed bowl, then beat in oil at room temperature.

Proportions: One large egg yolk with 1 tablespoon of vinegar will emulsify 3/4 cups of oil.

Light Custard Sauce

Description: A light-colored, creamy blend of egg yolks, milk and sugar that has been thickened by stirring together over moderate heat.

Use: This basic custard is used as filling and to coat desserts; it may be seasoned with vanilla, fruit, berries, caramalized sugar, etc.

Problem: The custard must be heated evenly to about 160°F in order to thicken.

Key Step: After the ingredients are all together, they are carefully heated enough to cause the custard to turn creamy, but not enough to cook the egg yolks.

Proportions: For 2 cups of custard: 1-3/4 cups of milk, 4 egg yolks, 1/2 cup of granulated sugar.

4

WORDS WITH TOO MUCH MEANING

INTRODUCTION TO CHAPTER 4: THE SIGNALS IN OUR SYNTAX

This chapter fulfills the promise, made in Chapter 1, to present "explicit instructions on how to...choose and arrange words to represent the thoughts we have in mind." Assuming that the thoughts in mind do result from Chapters 1, 2, and 3, this chapter becomes the demonstration for the circuit of concepts described in Chapter 1 and summarized under "Habits as Tools."

At this point that circuit of concepts stands in a situation analogous to that of an invention about to receive its first demonstration in a prototype machine. Both the circuit of concepts and the invention are to be tested by a demonstration; both the circuit of concepts and the invention involve novel approaches to established problems; and both demonstrations involve already familiar things, such as familiar words of English and familiar parts of the prototype machine. Experienced inventors will tell you that it is at this stage—the demonstration—that most inventions fail, and that these failures usually result from the failure of some conventional part of the prototype machine due to an overstrain imposed by the novel demands of the invention.

Reading this experience into our analogy, we might guess that the principles set forth in Chapters 1, 2, and 3 would overstrain some parts of English syntax, and that our choices of words and their arrangements should be adapted accordingly. This does not mean that the SPRI thought organization leads to a new language, like Esperanto; it means, rather, that users of SPRI need to concentrate on a few aspects of their vast intuitive knowledge of English syntax. We have a novel way to organize our thoughts and translate them into English prose; and we now approach the demonstration of that novel way.

Like good inventors, we should take nothing for granted; we should examine our machinery—our English—to be sure that it measures up to the purposes we are about to assign it. This is no small task. Even if this chapter included a complete book on English syntax, such as C. C. Fries's *The Structure of English*, or a complete book on clear and graceful writing, such as Graves and Hodge's *The Reader Over Your Shoulder*, that still would not be enough, because such books are general and our needs are specific. To resolve our present problem, we must test standard English syntax against our theses and discover what parts of that syntax are strained by our approach to prose. Then we can reinforce those points of strain with conscious understanding and allow the rest of our English syntax to follow along by force of habit. What is necessary is to find the points of strain.

Fortunately, those points of strain were revealed to me by chance through ten years with Henry Gordon, at the copy desk of *Chemical Engineering*. Henry worked in an unusual way, even for copy editors, who are usually gifted in terms of language. Unlike other copy editors, he was not expected to impose any style other than clarity. More important, he was not technically trained, and he insisted that he should not understand the contents of the articles he read. Because he did not understand the articles, he insisted that the magazine's editors sit with him while he read their manuscripts aloud. With the pages laid out on a typewriter table, he would settle himself in his chair, with the editor close on his right, and hunch forward as if making a physical effort; and he would read in a low voice. Although the meanings of many words were unknown to him, his voice would infallibly carry the proper inflections, obeying the rules of English syntax; and an editor could know immediately when the inflection did not match the intent of the prose. At times (sometimes too often) his voice would fade, and his hand would move toward the paper with his pencil almost in cadence with the inflections in his voice.

Since you have been through Chapters 1, 2, and 3, and are about to test those principles, you may imagine how I felt, many times, as I watched his pencil approach my manuscript. I wanted to object, to explain my reasons, or at least to discuss. But Henry would only stare at me, smiling politely, and when I paused for breath or his reaction, he would say, "Shall we go on?" And so we would go on reading. In effect, he acted as the unknown reader with whom an author can never argue. Either the language works—without additional explanation—or it fails.

However, I could take the manuscripts with Henry's markings back to my office and study them. After a while patterns could be detected; and those patterns indicated those rules of syntax that need to be consciously respected. Moreover, because a reader tends to ignore uncertainties and ambiguities if the thought comes out clearly, those rules, while not creating perfect grammar, are usually enough for clear prose. As we have seen, some thoughts can be signified by a single word, whereas others can only be represented by groups of words appearing as phrases, sentences, or even paragraphs. Altogether, those thoughts often exist like a cloud that forms a prognosis for a perception. However they must be strung out, when they are fitted to sequential words, in much the way that a strand of wool from a ball of fiber is strung out onto a spinning wheel. The many shorter pieces pull out others so that they overlap for an average part of their lengths. And from this, we see that the primary purpose of syntax is to overlap what we read now with that which went before. Which of the foregoing thoughts is fastened to this one? How do the others affect this connection? Is the connection strong enough to bring along other related thoughts? Readers automatically ask and answer these questions as they move through prose.

This calls for a type of thinking that moves with the speed of light to try to connect the verbal impressions—a thinking whose character conforms to the primitive mode of thought presented in Chapter 1. Take the sentence, "She's the man who tends our garden's mother." We can identify the signals that allow an average reader to bunch *the man who tends our garden's* into a single modifier equivalent to one word. First comes the word *the*, which is in the class of determiners to be looked at later. *The* signals that all to come between it and a subsequent noun is a modifier. Thus when we say *the glass eye*, the word *glass* is a modifier and the word *eye* is its noun. In the case of *the man*, the word *man* could be our noun, but we have a carry-over from *She is*; we know that a *man* is not a *she*, so our primitive mind says to wait, and we go on. Next comes the word *who*, which signals that the next group of words will contain a verb and modify *man*. Sure enough, we get *tends our garden*, so that we see *the man who tends our garden* as a single symbol. Then the addition of the possessive, *'s*, to the word *garden* reflects not back to *garden* but back to *man*, so that the following word *mother* is understood as the man's mother. If we refer back to "Mental Tools: Levels of Thought, Concepts, Uncertainty," in Chapter

1, we can see how our primitive mode of thinking could only perform this marvelous feat by making the words labile, rigid, diffuse, syncretic, and indefinite.

I am not going to mess around with something as powerful and as useful as our primitive mode of thinking. Rather, we should all recognize it for the precious thing it is, and hope that our readers are well equipped with it. On the other hand, Henry Gordon was demonstrating a most highly developed primitive mode of thinking as he read my manuscripts, so we might assume that his corrections represent those specific syntactic signals where his primitive mode was strained. Thus his corrections are comparable to the linguistic analysis made by C. C. Fries in *The Structure of English*, as well as the empirical rules articulated by Graves and Hodge in *The Reader Over Your Shoulder*. We can reduce our observations to four general rules or principles: (1) the importance of putting words and phrases in the proper order; (2) the importance of 154 words that act as signals; (3) the effect of a thought, or prognosis, on words and phrases as they occur in the written sequence; and (4) the effect of a few signals that overreach other signals, and accordingly are suitable for conscious attention.

ORDERLINESS WITH ENGLISH

The most provocative type of correction that Henry brought to my manuscripts was transpositions. Putting his pencil point to the paper, he would carefully draw a line underneath word after word of a group of words and isolate them with two short lines drawn vertically from the underline up through the line of type. Then, with an arrow curving out through the margin and back between two words of the text, he would indicate that the underlined group of words should be moved to that position. The groups of words included sentences, clauses, or phrases; they represented thoughts or important parts of thoughts; and they usually involved a thought structure that had been put together according to the principles of Chapters 2 and 3. However, Henry did not try to understand the thoughts, so that notions of uncertainty, purpose, ambiguity, and so on, were not considered for the textual arrangements. And because Henry's transpositions sounded better, they became parts of articles that were published and favorably accepted in readership surveys. Consequently, if thoughts were to be organized in a way to make the composition more interesting, that organization needed first to suit the grammar.

Eventually, comparisons of many transpositions revealed that clear grammatical syntax did not depend on the organization of thoughts so much as on the signals that identified the thoughts; when Henry moved a word group, it was not because of its location but because of my grammatical failure to signal the desired location. Once I realized this, it was relatively easy to locate the needed signals in Fries's *The Structure of English*. Because of their importance, these signals are worth segregating out of our thoughts of intuitively known grammatical signals for conscious use and attention. All of these signals are words, which are used so much that they have lost their lexical meanings, and operate only as signals. Generally, three categories of these signal words are involved, according to whether the signal is for (1) a modifying word group, (2) an included sentence, or (3) a connected sentence.

Signals for modifying word-groups. These word signals are among those identified as "function words" by Fries and classified as "Group F" within the function words. There are thirteen of them, all worth memorizing: *at, by, from, in, of, on, to, with, for, over, up, across,* and *after*. Although some of these thirteen words have other functions, their use as signals for word-group modifiers is so common that they can be discovered scattered through almost any text. For example, the beginning of Chapter 3 is repeated below with these signal words italicized. Before reviewing these examples, however, you should be aware that conventional grammars will confuse this group of signal words with many labels derived from subjectively assigned meanings. By contrast to the conventional, your purpose will be accomplished through simply noting the thirteen words and remembering that they all signal word-group modifiers.

This chapter fulfills the promise, made *in* Chapter 1, *to* present "explicit instructions *on* how to . . . assemble thoughts *for* easy and interesting reading." That fulfilled promise is accompanied *by* some notions picked up *in* Chapters 1 and 2. Among those is the notion that professional people do considerable thinking beyond the thinking they normally express *by* speaking and writing. Evidence *of* this notion has been available *for* years *in* legal case records, graphs, mathematical formulae, computer programs, and creatively designed objects, all of which give evidence *of* thought that is not expressed *in* words and sentences. Yet almost all treatises *on* English composition assume, like the French writer Nicolas Boileau-Despereaux (1636–1711), that that which is well understood is clearly expressed, as well as the converse, that that which is poorly expressed is poorly understood.

The word-group modifiers and their objects are as follows:

- *in Chapter 1* (modifies *made*)
- *to present "explicit instructions* (modifies *promise*)
- *on how to assemble* (modifies *instructions*)
- *for easy and interesting reading"* (modifies *assemble*)
- *by some notions* (modifies *accompanied*)

- *in Chapters 1 and 2* (modifies *picked up*)
- *by speaking and writing* (modifies *express*)
- *of this notion* (modifies *evidence*)
- *in legal case records, graphs, mathematical formulae, computer programs, and creatively designed objects* (modifies *available*)
- *of thought* (modifies *evidence*)
- *in words and sentences* (modifies *expressed*)
- *on English composition* (modifies *treatises*)

And in the first sentence of the next paragraph comes the expression, "... an occupational hazard *to* professional people working *in* research, law, teaching, and similar fields...." Indeed, this type of modifier is so common that one has been used to introduce the last example, because this paragraph began, "And *in the first sentence*...." Furthermore, this last example reveals something interesting about these modifiers. Note that the phrase *in the first sentence* modifies the verb *comes*; and that this verb precedes the noun it acts for, *expression*, so that the sentence is inverted. We thus observe that these word-group modifiers can not reach across a head noun to a modified verb, or across a head verb to a modified noun.

All of these word-group modifiers exhibit a structural meaning of identification or description. Thus they are particularly useful in texts that use word symbols to identify specific concepts. For example, under "Sources of Uncertainty" in Chapter 3, the description that assigns a purpose to the abstraction, *baseball*, needs careful identification of the terms, so we have...

...two teams *of nine players each*, the winning of which is decided *by the number of* "*runs*" each team has made *by the end of a legal game.*

In this example, the signal word *of* has introduced a modifier of the noun *teams*, as *nine players each*; the first signal word *by* has introduced a modifier of the verb *decided*, as *number of runs*; and the second *by* has introduced a modifier of the verb *has made*, as *the end of a legal game*.

Generally, as the point of view or purpose of a text becomes less abstract and more restrictive, the composition calls for more precise identification and description of the terms. This usually means more word-group modifiers and a more intensive use of the Group F signal words, as is illustrated in the description of baseball that assigns a purpose to the batter: "player *on a baseball team*... imbedded *in the ground at his feel*... hurled *by a pitcher*... cross home plate *at a level between his shoulders and knees*... 'walk' *to his first 'base'*...," and so forth.

Signals for included sentences. These signal words are Group J of Fries's 154 identified function words. There are sixteen of them: *when, whenever, because, since, so, therefore, although, but, nevertheless, before, after, and, whether, which, that,* and *where.* Although some of these words appear in other groups of function words, their most important use, with respect to thought syntax, consists in signalling an included sentence. To illustrate, consider the last sentence of the first paragraph of Chapter 3 repeated above.

...that *which is well understood is clearly expressed,...*
...that *which is poorly expressed is poorly understood.*

In both of these included sentences, the signal word *which* acts as a subject; and herein lies an important principle for English composition. Because the signal words for an included sentence act both as head of the included sentence and as modifier of some word in the main sentence, the location of these signal words is critical. The last sentence of the third paragraph in Chapter 3 illustrates the problems to be dealt with:

Because such activities are performed without even the silent egocentric speech studied by psychologists, the act of ordering up words to express the thoughts in the absence of the actions is difficult.

You should perhaps reread that entire paragraph in order to decide for yourself whether or not your reading was disturbed by some ambiguity. The sample sentence uses a construction that is repeated throughout this book and is something of a gamble. Only you can know from your reading if the gamble worked. That sentence could have been written as follows:

The act of ordering up words to express the thoughts in the absence of the actions is difficult, because such activities are performed without even the silent egocentric speech studied by psychologists.

With this alternative arrangement, it is clear that *because* modifies *difficult;* and this is not clear in the previous version. However a problem arises in the revised version with respect to *such activities.* Because the intuitive tendency is to refer such modifiers to the nearest preceding object, this arrangement causes *such activities* to refer to *the act of ordering up.* This is wrong and confusing, because the intended object is *classifying and filing documents, using a telephone, or choosing clothes,* which appears in the previous sentence of the paragraph. Thus the alternative arrangement would require repeating the mention of those activities. This could be done, as follows:

The act of ordering up words to express the thoughts in the absence of the actions is difficult, because thoughtful activities are usually performed without even the silent egocentric speech studied by psychologists.

However, there were other reasons for avoiding this construction. First, it gives too much attention to *silent egocentric speech studied by psychologists*. Although many readers may not have read about egocentric speech, I felt that to discuss it would be a digression, so I gambled that adding *silent* would make the words self-explanatory, and opted for an arrangement that would put them in a less prominent position. Second, I wanted to emphasize the notion of *difficult*, and this could be done by locating that word far from its modifier. This causes the signal word *because* to exert its maximum, telling the reader that an included sentence is to follow and that somewhere after this is a modified word. The word *difficult* thus has high information content.

Another example of included sentences is found in the quote from Adelbert Ames, Jr., the last sentence of the first paragraph under "Sources of Uncertainty." The signal word *but* is used to indicate this included sentence, as follows:

> The degree of the similarity can vary, *but* we can never know the inherent nature of objects and their relationships as such.

In this construction, the word *but* modifies the word *vary* by putting a limit on it; and through *vary* the included sentence following *but* reaches all the way back to the preceding sentence, which it confirms: "At best their [sensations and events] relationship can only be a similarity or analogy." Now, what if the included sentence had been signalled by the word *however*, which appears later as a signal for connected sentences?

> The degree of this similarity can vary. However, we can never know the inherent nature of objects and their relationships as such.

I feel that the subtle thought has lost something with the weakening of the link, from *but* to *however*. On the other hand, what if *but* were replaced by *although*?

> Although we can never know the inherent nature of objects and their relationships as such, the degree of this similarity can vary.

You will have to decide if this inversion puts too much strain on *this similarity* and the words *be a similarity* appearing in the previous sentence. If your reading pace was interrupted by that strain, this inverted version does not work; if the sentence read smoothly, then this version puts the most emphasis on the word *vary*.

Given the thought, how would you express it? It is in making such choices that you will find your personal style, which will be a style of thinking as much as a style of writing. Both the above construction ending in *vary*, as well as the foregoing example ending in *difficult*, provide examples of the emphasis that can be obtained with heightened information, when the appearance of a signalled complement is delayed until the end of the sentence. If your taste in composition runs to series of statements each related only by an overriding idea, these constructions may be worth studying and using. If one wanted to articulate the difficulties of putting words to thought, or the varieties of relation between sensation and perception, these constructions offer the opportunity. For example, the text with *difficult* in it might have gone on as follows:

> Because such activities are performed without even the silent egocentric speech studied by psychologists, the act of ordering up words to express the thoughts is difficult. Words must be found to replace the movements and percepts representing thoughts. However, those movements and percepts are made without symbols; they can not be remembered unless the situation is repeated; and with no memory of the parts of the activity, there is nothing to which the words can be attached.

Signals for connected sentences. There seem to be more ways for signalling connected sentences than almost any other grammatical construct. My own use of these signals developed through three distinct stages. First, Henry Gordon brought a lot of transpositions to my manuscripts. I tried to avoid those partly with greater use of word signals for connected sentences. But then, as the number of transpositions decreased, he began to circle the signal words and politely ask if I felt a strong need for them. Somehow, that embarrassed me, as if I had been caught cheating. I struggled to reduce the number of connecting signals without getting into transpositions again. Finally, as he was putting the papers together after a reading one day, he remarked that my manuscripts were unusually "clean." What satisfaction! In any event, even if you only put them in to later delete them, the signal words for connected sentences are worth conscious attention. There are four groups of them: (1) substitutions for nouns; (2) combinations with *this*, *that*, *else*, and *other*; (3) some adverbs; and (4) the familiar conjunctions.

The substitutions for nouns are compared with Group A function words in the table with that listing. They are illustrated below with excerpts from this text.

From the beginning of Chapter 3:

That promise is accompanied by some notions picked up in Chapters 1 and 2. Among *those* is the notion that professional people do considerable thinking...

From the fourth paragraph of Chapter 3:

Exactly because they do believe writing and thought are synonymous, commercial writers do not undertake the problem of putting words to specific non-verbal thoughts. Instead *they* adapt the thought to the words.

Typically, John begins: "In the beginning was the Word; and the Word was with God; and the Word was God" (John 1:1). And then *he* proceeds to write the fourth Gospel of the New Testament.

From the last paragraph before "Sources of Uncertainty," in Chapter 3:

And the proof of our analogy has been that it works. *It* has transformed a vague problem into a search for specific uncertainty...

As a final example, from the sixth paragraph under "Sources of Uncertainty":

These two kinds of purpose, abstract and active, show where to look for and use uncertainty in organizing prose.
This can be demonstrated practically through three...

The second group of signals for connected sentences refer a following noun to the previous sentence, and thus do not stand alone for the noun. These also appear in the table of substitutes with Group A. Some examples are as follows.
From the second paragraph of Chapter 3:

Yet almost all treatises on English composition assume, like the French writer Nicolas Boileau-Despereaux (1636–1711) that that which is well understood is clearly expressed, as well as the converse, that that which is poorly expressed is poorly understood.
This false assumption represents an occupational...

From the eighth paragraph in Chapter 3:

If the analogy is good, some of the rules of the mathematical constructs should also apply to the relations between prose and non-verbal thinking—rules such as the following:

These rules seem reasonable and...

From the second paragraph under "Sources of Uncertainty" in Chapter 3:

It is as if nature had set about to create a super hoax with humans, like donkeys chasing a "feed bag." But we are in *that situation* as long as...

From the subsequent two paragraphs:

It is only when we recognize that so-called facts and truths in themselves are not the ultimate goal, but have value in so far as they show us the ever becoming reality and contribute to our purposes, that we shall cease to be hoaxed.
This observation explains some of the elusiveness inherent in action-based, non-verbal thinking.

The third group of words signalling connected sentences are some adverbs; these are: *then, afterward, hereafter, thereafter, henceforth, hitherto, heretofore, meantime, meanwhile, later,* and *earlier*. Because this type of connective signal is usually found in spoken language and descriptions, it is not illustrated with examples.

The fourth group of signals are the conjunctions, which are already familiar to users of English, so that we only need to list all fourteen of them: *however, yet, nevertheless, also, moreover, besides, likewise, otherwise, therefore, thus, consequently, accordingly, furthermore,* and *similarly*.

This list of conjunctions completes the important syntactical devices that can be used to signal related thoughts or parts of thoughts in English. Thus the key signal for relating one thought to another is a word; and orderliness in English depends on a different approach to words. Instead of occupying part of a vocabulary of words with fixed meanings, these words are independently existing, separate objects, part of a large group of signal words to be reviewed next.

SIGNAL WORDS WITH NO MEANING

All native speakers of a language possess an intuitive skill with which they can give verbal expression to a thought. Most native speakers will also have received some sort of instruction in their language, through which their intuitive skills are supposed to be guided and improved, and through which their language is made to conform to an accepted standard. Accordingly, most native speakers will have learned "grammar," in the guise of names for different kinds of words and parts of speech, along with rules for applying these different words and parts of speech. Unfortunately, almost all conventional grammar assumes a knowledge of the total meaning, in order to arrive at an identification of the word class, speech part, and rule. Thus in the sentence, *The man gave the boy the money*, the words *man*, *boy*, and *money* are called "nouns" as well as "subject," "indirect object," and "object," respectively. Yet none of these labels can be applied without a prior understanding of the sentence.

This approach to language is acceptable as long as we assume that thought and language are synonymous. If we have learned to compose written prose by, first, putting words on paper, then reviewing (editing) those words to see what about them we like and what they suggest, and then revising and adding accordingly, we can obtain much benefit from a grammatical analysis that assumes knowledge of the total meaning. Because we do not quite know what we intend to say until we see it in words, each sentence is its own justification.

However, if we approach writing already in possession of thoughts for which we want to find an adequate expression in words, the conventional grammar is like putting the cart (words) before the horse (meaning); and the conventional grammar is wrong, less than useless. In a thoughtful approach, we must fit words and structures of words to our ideas in exactly the same fashion that a mathematician or computer programmer designs equations and algorithms to fit his or her ideas. The emphasis is on form. Just as the form of an equation determines the shape of a curve of a correlation, so does the form of language give shape to a verbalized thought. We need to know just what form of the language best suits the form of a specific idea or relation of ideas.

Fortunately, most of us have an intuitive feel for much of the form of our language; and it is only when we attempt the more difficult thoughts that we need help from a conscious knowledge. But we will not find such help in the conventional grammar; instead we must find it in a linguistic approach based on the form of the language and not its meaning. One such analysis is *The Structure of English*, by C. C. Fries. Fries describes for non-linguists the results of a scientifically rigorous linguistic approach to the analysis of English. Using fifty hours of telephone conversation taped in Ann Arbor, Michigan, he divided the conversation into separate utterances and analyzed them according to their forms, in much the same manner that one might crack a code or decipher an unknown language. His principal analytic device was substitution. Taking minimum free utterances as frames, for example, he substituted words in the different parts of those frames. Three such frames were

The concert was good.
The clerk remembered the tax.
The team went there.

The structural parts of those frames are occupied by four classes of words: (1) the part occupied by *concert, clerk, tax,* and *team*; (2) the part occupied by *was, remembered,* and *went*; (3) the part occurring between *the* and *concert, clerk,* or *team*; and (4) the part occupied by *there*. The positions in the frames thus distinguish the four classes of words. For example, "The good concert was there" works, whereas "The there concert was good" does not; and the substitution has shown the different classes occupied by *there* and *good*.

Fries's method of analysis brings to English syntax many observations that are not available through conventional grammar. Those observations are useful for teaching English, for information analysis, and for computer programming. However, many of them need not be pointed out to writers who know and use them untuitively. The outstanding exception is a group of words that did not fit into any of the four standard positions of the frame sentences. Because of this and because those words have no lexical meanings, they exist as separate items. They are, of course, known by every user of English, but not in the roles that Fries has empirically discovered. In those roles, they function not as words but as part of the sentence frame; and they thus give a structural meaning equivalent to the sentence structure. There are fifteen kinds of such structural words, each kind a subgroup of the overall group, which Fries called "function" words. The fifteen groups, lettered *A* through *O*, will be described essentially as he presented them.

Group A. These are words that could be substituted for *the* in the frame sentences. They are: *the, a/an, every, no, my, our, your, her, his, their, each, all, both, some, any, few, more, most, much, many, its, John's, this/these, that/those, one, two, three, four, five, eighteen, twenty, thirty-one* (up to *ninety-nine*).

We've already seen how some of these words can signal a connected sentence, and have compared them with substitutes for Fries's class 1 words, or nouns, in the table. Fries made his studies of these words around 1948–1950. Some seven years later, Heinz Werner presented his study, *Comparative Psychology of Mental Development* (1957), with its identification of primitive and cognitive modes of thought. Thus it has been after Fries made his linguistic study that we have been able to identify the Group A function words as signals for communication in the primitive mode, as shown under "Verbal Tools: Logic and Concepts" in Chapter 1. On the other hand, it was in 1948 that C. E. Shannon introduced modern information theory with his comments about the vast knowledge carried by every speaker of a language. One can not help but wonder what Shannon might have done with the detailed data available from Fries, or how Fries might have used Werner's concepts of primitive and cognitive to interpret the structural meanings discussed in *The Structure of English*. The average user of English has intuitive knowledge of many signals that mean "modifier to come," or equally mean "think primitively"; and we have seen in several examples how an extended passage of primitively received words adds to the information content of the cognitively received words that follow. However, our purpose here is to use English, not to study it; so it is enough to be aware of the Group A words and their signals.

Group B. Put the frame sentences in both the present and past tenses and discover which words can be located immediately before the verb. These words are: *may, might, can, could, will, would, should, must, has, has to, had, was, got, kept, had to, did, be, keep, get.*

Group C. Substitution in the location immediately after the verb or a Group B word revealed one word, *not*, which signals a negative interpretation of the following modifier.

Group D. Substitutions into the positions immediately before adjectives and adverbs produced lists of words, some of which could occur before all types of adjectives, others that occur only before adjectives of comparison, like *better*, and still others that occur before adverbs.

Those occurring before adjectives are: *very, quite, awfully, really, awful, real, any, pretty, too, fairly, more, rather,* and *most*. Those that occur before adjectives of comparison are: *still, even, much, some,* and *no*. Those occurring before adverbs are: *way, really, more, less, more or less, almost, right, very, quite, pretty, rather, awfully, mighty, too, much, still, even, no, right,* and *just*.

Examples are:

The concert was *very* good.

The concert was *even* better.

The concert was *still* better *much* later.

Group E. These words, which can occur between two similar parts of speech, are: *and, or, not, nor, but, rather than*. Examples are:

The concert, *not* the lecture, was good.

The concert *and* the lecture were good.

Also included in this group are words that can appear before the first of the parts thus joined. These are: *both, either, neither,* and *not*.

Group F. These were identified under "Orderliness in English" as signals for modifying word groups. They are revealed by ascertaining which words can be substituted right after the lead noun when several nouns precede the verb. They are: *at, by, for, from, in, of, on, to, with, over, up, across,* and *after*. An example is:

Comparing Group A Function Words with Noun-Substitutes Signalling Connected Sentences

	Substitutes Signalling Connected Sentences		
Group A Function Words	*Group A Substitutes*	*Substitutes of Other Types of Words*	
the		others	another
a/an		lots	several
every			which
no	none		what
my	mine	I	who
our	ours	we	whichever
your	yours	you	whatever
her	hers	she	
his	his	he	
their	theirs	they	
each	each		
all	all		
both	both		
some	some		
any	any		
few	few		
more	more		
most	most		
many	many		
much			
its		it	
this/these	this/these		
that/those	that/those		
one	one		
eighteen	eighteen		

The concert *at* the school was good.

Group G. This one word signals "verb coming," and appears in three different forms resembling the declensions of a verb: *do, does, did.* In addition to signalling such uses as, "The good concert *does* not take place today," it can also be injected to reinforce the verb that comes after a modifier, as in the second sentence of this chapter:

Assuming that the thoughts in mind *do* result from Chapters 1, 2, and 3...

Group H. This one signal word looks the same as, but is easily distinguished from, an adverb. It is *there,* as in "*There* is a good concert today."

Group I. Although some of these words appear in Group J, their signal, when used as part of this group, is that of a question. They are: *when, why, where, how, who, which, what.*

Group J. These words signal included sentences, as discussed under "Orderliness in English." Again, they are: *after, when, whenever, because, although, since, before, so, nevertheless, therefore, and, but.*

Group K. These words usually occur in spoken English, where they signal a response. They are: *well, oh, now, why.* The word *now* can also be used in written compositions to signal a comment on a foregoing thought, as at the beginning of the seventh paragraph of Chapter 3:

Now, our purpose in making this analogy is to discover if there is indicated some relation between verbal and non-verbal thought.

Group L. These well-known signals occur almost exclusively in spoken language. They are: *yes, no.*

Group M. These signals resemble the signals of Group K, except that they act more to signal a call for attention. They are: *say, listen, look.*

Group N. This well-known signal is *please.*

Group O. These words exert a signal similar to *please,* except that they indicate inclusion of the speaker or writer. They are: *let us, let's.*

In that these words account for about one-third of the English words spoken and written; that they differ from the ordinary words of the English vocabulary by having no lexical meaning; that they function like the sentence structure to signal such things as mode of thought, questions, and response; and that they therefore exist as separate items apart from the rest of the language, they should be worth the time it takes to get familiar with them and their meanings in these fifteen empirically determined groupings.

Armed with conscious knowledge of these signals plus the previously described signals, one might reasonably feel ready to set about mastering English composition. However, there remains the junction at which thought and syntax come together. This junction has been studied as "semantics"; however, we will consider it as "meaning," specifically lexical meaning. How do our composition and our syntax affect what is meant by the words in our vocabulary?

MEANING IS WHERE YOU FIND IT

Unfortunately, any time a composition is interesting and satisfying, that composition has been the product of aggressively creative hard work. Many surveys of successful writers show almost unanimous agreement that the ease of reading is directly proportional to the effort of composing. The best that a writer can do is to make sure that this necessary effort is not misdirected and wasted; and a first step toward a well-directed effort consists of separating one's point of view from that of the reader.

Whereas a reader can be expected to try not to notice ambiguities, a successful writer must keep constantly alert to every one of them—to implications in thought, to the use of signals in grammar, and to the use of emphasis by means of construction. This all converges on an unavoidable need to give close consideration to the meaning of words, which might indicate a need for lexicography. Choose precise words according to their dictionary meanings, and make use of a large precise vocabulary. However, it does not help a writer to know a word if the readers do not know that word, so the lexicographic approach can not be said to lead to clear writing.

Ordinary words do not necessarily mean what we want them to mean. This is no small problem, as is illustrated by the frame sentence, "The concert was good." We have seen how words can be classified by substituting them into different positions in that sentence, but we have not asked just what that sentence means. Although a reader might accept that sentence as merely a statement of fact, a writer should note that the sentence is ambiguous. Since the sentence is part of a telephone conversation, and since use of the Group A word, *the*, signals that this concert has been mentioned previously, any ambiguity around *concert* may come from lifting the sentence out of its context. However, similar assumptions can not be made for the word *good*. Just what is meant by the word *good*? A careful writer will recognize that its meaning is ambiguous. Unhappily, further consideration shows that this ambiguity about *good* is only typical of many modifiers that can be put in the frame sentence in the same position. For example, the words *educational, fine, clear, important, singular, difficult, easy, different*, and so forth can be substituted for *good*, but what exactly does each mean? Considering these words in that manner, we might feel we could respond to each of them like Alice in *Alice in Wonderland*, when she said, "Somehow, it seems to fill my head with ideas—only I don't exactly know what they are." She was responding to the Jabberwocky's poem:

> Twas brillig, and the slithy toves
>   Did gyre and gimble in the wabe;
> All mimsy were the borogroves,
>   And the mome raths outgrabe...

Although the effect of the frame sentence is not so intense as the Jabberwocky's poem, it amounts to the same thing—clear syntax and an ambiguous lexical meaning. The comparison demonstrates the need for writers to know something about the lexical meanings of common words—the possibilities and how to choose among those possibilities.

By coincidence, it is possible to begin with the word *good*. Not only does it figure prominently in one of Fries's frame sentences, it has also been studied by another student of language, Paul Ziff in *Semantic Analysis*. While working on a manuscript on aesthetics, Ziff decided it would be helpful to be able to say, at least roughly, what was meant by the phrase *good painting*. He solved this problem in a manner welcome to most technical people—empirically. Taking 160 sentences, such as "The concert was good," he determined what was meant by each, and he put all those meanings together for the concluding statement of his study:

There are variations on the theme, but this is what "good" means: answering to certain interests.[1]

Although Ziff's definition may displease people who seek moral implications for *good*, it provides writers with an opening through which they can pass to a vast array of useful analogies and associations between words and what they mean in a sentence. The definition *answering to certain interests* is at once vague and specific. It is left vague by the word *certain*, and made specific by the word *interests*, provided we understand *interests* as indicating purpose and a prognosis. Although we do not have time for a similar study of similar words, we can divide the meanings of similar words into two parts, one vague and one specific. Taking "answering to certain interests" to the frame sentence, "The concert was good," that word *good* can now be construed as "answering to certain interests." To avoid being ambiguous, a careful writer might therefore define those interests, or purposes, by using some of the syntax signals discussed earlier, as for example:

The concert was good with Professor Hardwell conducting.

In this sentence, the word *good* is qualified with a word-group modifier introduced by the signal word *with*. However, a closer look reveals that this modifier affects the meaning of the word *good* only by amplifying the meaning of the word *concert*; there is still no precise identification of those "interests."

The following sentences, which modify *good* with connected sentences, do articulate those "interests," as for a well-coordinated orchestra and for the inclusion of music by Britten and Shostakovich:

The concert was good because Professor Hardwell kept the musicians under close control.

The concert was good because it included music by Britten and Shostakovich.

There are further possibilities:

Because Professor Hardwell kept the musicians under close control, the concert was good. The violins sounded as one instrument; the timing of the tympanist was perfect; and the swelling crescendos in Berlioz's "Symphony Fantastique" were in unison and not overdone.

At this point, we begin to have some understanding of what was meant by the word *good*. Also, at this point, careful writers might have some worrisome questions plaguing their consciousnesses, questions such as: Do I want to give that much description? Does the reader want to know that much? Does this precise information offer any useful analogies? The answers to those questions must be specific to the particular use of the word in question; the decision on how to proceed must be personal; and that decision will be the essence of a personal style.

The use of any one of a large number of words with ambiguous meaning, such as *good*, serves to introduce uncertainty. A writer should decide, first, if the uncertainty is wanted; and if it is not wanted, that word should be replaced by a word with a more precise lexical meaning. If the uncertainty is wanted, it can be dealt with by one of the methods just shown. This text has dealt with the same problem. You have gone through this text as a reader. Now, you can reconsider it as a writer, and perhaps decide how you would handle the same problems to suit your taste. Refer back to "Signals for included sentences" under "Orderliness in English," to the indented sentence that reads as follows:

Because such activities are performed without even the silent egocentric speech studied by psychologists, the act of ordering up words to express the thoughts in the absence of the actions is difficult.

You were asked to decide if that sentence was unsatisfactorily ambiguous, and you were offered an inversion that put the modifying clause, beginning with *because*, right next to the modified word *difficult*. Now, you can consider a more subtle question, one that should stand as an archetype for the problem of meaning and help you make conscious answers to that type of problem for yourself. Consider that word *difficult*. Like *good*, it can be substituted in the frame sentence; and like *good*, it has no fixed lexical meaning. Consider the sentence offered in the revised version as follows:

The act of ordering up words to express the thoughts in the absence of the actions is difficult, because the thoughtful activities are usually performed without even the silent egocentric speech of the psychologists.

You will see that the connected sentence beginning with *because* does not further define *difficult*, except by defining the act of ordering up. This approach to solving ambiguity is closely analogous to the sentence, "The concert was good with Professor Hardwell conducting." In your own reading and writing, you will be confronted with other examples of this analogy thousands of times. Now turn back to "Signals for included sentences," look three paragraphs after the above repeated example, and you will find a version in which *difficult* is defined in terms of words to replace movements, which are ephemeral. Note that this statement is closely analogous to the last elaboration of "The concert was good." For a more tenuous, but still valid, analogy, now consider again the quote from Proust, which we saw in Chapter 3.

Many years ago, I would go to bed early. Sometimes, as I snuffed my candle, my eyes closed so fast I didn't have time to say to myself, "I'm going to sleep." And half an hour later, the thought that it was time to go to sleep would wake me; I wanted to lay aside the book I imagined in my hands and to blow out the light; it seemed that I myself was the thing written about: a church, a quartet, the rivalry between Francis I and Charles V. This belief would last during several wakeful seconds; it didn't seem unreasonable, but weighed like scales on my eyes and kept them from realizing that the candle wasn't lit.

Note that all of the text following "And half an hour later" serves to modify the meaning of "my eyes closed so fast." Would you, as a writer, be satisfied with, "I didn't have time to say to myself, 'I'm going to sleep' "? Or would your taste tend toward a construction resembling that of Proust?

When you have considered these methods of dealing with meaning, you have passed over a threshold of transformation from reader to writer. This transformation holds utmost significance for your approach to writing, so do not lose track of it. Go back and forth several times, first reader, then writer, then reader, and so forth. Remember that you will need to play the role of reader when you edit your own writing, so that the reader you learn to be will become a part of your writing. When you've exhausted the above comparisons, turn to some other writing that you like. Discover the approaches to meaning following in that writing; and thus discover those approaches that appeal most to you as a reader. You may lose your enjoyment of those texts, but what you gain in knowledge of your own tastes and how to suit them will be well worth the loss.

Of course, words like *good* and *difficult* are typical of only a part of our vocabulary; and they can be differentiated from other words and expressions, such as *copper, concrete, symphony, water, north, summer,* and so forth. A writer can relate these meaningful words with the cognitive mode of thinking, and the ambiguous words, like *good*, with the primitive mode. Thus it is sometimes good to force more significance into a statement, albeit ambiguously, with a simple statement, such as, "The concert was good." For example, get *The Sun Also Rises*, by Ernest Hemingway, and read his descriptions of traveling by bus and fishing in the Pyrenees. Once you, as a writer, know where you prefer to concentrate your meaning, you will have your own style—a style that is even suited to publishing in the professional journals.

A HIERARCHY OF SIGNALS

Consider once again those sample sentences involving *good*.

The concert was good with Professor Hardwell conducting.

The concert was good because Professor Hardwell kept the musicians under close control.

The first of these two samples used the Group F word, *with*, to introduce a modifying word group; the second used the Group J word, *because*, to introduce an included sentence. The difference is reflected in the different forms of the verb, the modifying word group using an *-ing* form, *conducting*, while the included sentence uses an active form, *kept*. These concordances are part of the English speakers' vast intuitive knowledge that has been passed over, not needing conscious attention. Unfortunately, that may have given an unintentional inference that the function words are dominating in a hierarchy of syntax signals. Many conventional grammars do present English syntax in terms of structural hierarchies. However, this implies that a writer has the ability to direct thoughts by means of the dominant signals; and both the view of syntax as a hierarchy and the implication are wrong. A syntax signal can no more bend the direction of thought than a road sign can change the direction of a road. Signal and sign both show an already existing direction. Such a distinction is critical in composing complex texts.

The agreement between parts of syntax is explained through the concept of the primitive mode of thought. Because the primitive mode is labile, rigid, syncretic, diffuse, and indefinite, and because it is fast as light, our primitive minds are able to withhold an interpretation, keeping the precise meanings of the parts of a statement in a suspended, meaningless cloud until all the cues are in. Then the system gels; each part assumes its significance as part of the whole; and each unit combines with the others to form a unified meaning that is something different from a mere adding up of the parts. This action is fundamental to language; without the primitive mode of thinking, we would not be able to speak, write, understand spoken language, or read. The only way to describe the concordance imposed by the primitive mode is to consider the signals as equivalent and compatible. This view then lets us understand how faulty grammar is often automatically corrected by the reader or listener, or, when that is impossible, how it causes an intense feeling of frustration and annoyance.

Within this grand structure, there are two concording features that, perhaps uniquely in English, can be used to bring together long passages of loosely associated thought, and that are almost always available for the complex texts about professional thoughts. These depend on that property of English, outstanding among languages, to be free of concordances among forms of the words. We do not change the verb to accommodate the differences between person and tense, as for example the French do, when they assign some 108 different forms to the single verb, *aimer*. Nor do we classify our nouns according to masculine and feminine and assign corresponding endings to the associated modifiers. In fact, when we consider all of the concordances that are necessary to other languages but not required in English, one might wonder how we make ourselves understood to each other.

Because English does not require many concordances among words, that burden of consistency falls to only two features: agreements between singulars and plurals, and the order of subject and verb. Because the other special forms for tense and gender are omitted, the concordance between plurals, or between singulars, becomes extremely powerful; and because there are no special concording forms to link them, a subject and its verb occur in only two possible arrangements: The verb after the subject (statement), and the verb or its surrogate before the subject (question). A writer does well to stay alert to these two requirements. Their evidence is so common as to beg specific examples, other than to reread this paragraph or any other paragraph in this text.

FEEDBACK

Like Chapters 1, 2, and 3, this chapter begins with an analogy. In Chapter 1, the analogy was a comparison between a sugar house and other forms of non-verbal thought; in Chapter 2, it was a comparison between the thinking required for design and prose compositions; in Chapter 3, it was a comparison between the mathematics of uncertainty and verbal articulation; and in this chapter, an analogy with an invention's prototype was made to SPRI composition. In this last case, the analogy suggested that an emphasis on SPRI composition might bring distinct strains to English syntax, and those distinct strains were conformed through the pattern of corrections made by a copy editor.

A distinctive pattern of errors demanded a distinctive grammatical analysis to understand and correct the errors. However, conventional English grammars did not provide this. The conventional approach to English grammar is based on definitions and rules derived from a prior understanding of the meanings of the words analyzed. These were not suitable for SPRI composition, because SPRI composition does not assign words a prior meaning; it does not find its thought in words, but finds words to suit the thought. Consequently the lack of an appropriate grammar might have stopped SPRI composition had it not been for the existence of an accepted, scientifically rigorous analysis based on linguistic principles emphasizing form rather than prior meaning.

This linguistic analysis not only offered the means for understanding the errors typical of SPRI composition, but it showed that correcting those errors could be simplified to the use of a few dozen meaningless function words. Because these function words hold no lexical meaning, they operate as structural parts of sentences, where they are easily identified. Compared to the syntactical signals of word order, prefixes, suffixes, and so on, and their combinations, the few dozen function words are infinitely easier to commit to conscious understanding. And because native users of English already carry an intuitive knowledge of the infinitely complex signals, a conscious understanding of the function words offers the writer an extremely powerful tool for molding sentences to fit complex thoughts.

It is possible to locate a function word with its word group right next to the modified word, or at the opposite end of the sentence. It was shown that, by introducing a sentence with a function word and its word group, the meaning of that word group can be held in suspense up to a point at which all those words unload their meanings as a single unit onto the modified word. The manner in which readers perform the necessary feats of understanding can be explained through the primitive mode of thought. The effects of unloading all that meaning onto the single modified word are explained through information theory. The overall result is a practical method through which the forms of sentences can be altered to have them more closely reflect a given thought.

However, this method of heightening meaning has brought attention to a new source of ambiguity, which is an integral part of our language. Many words resemble the word *good* in that they serve the same formal function and, like *good*, do not have a precise lexical meaning. When function words are used to concentrate the meanings of a word group onto a single modified word with no clear lexical meaning, the result is emphatic ambiguity. This can be used as an excuse for further discourse. More importantly, it presents the conscious writer with a choice about how far he or she wants to go into details; and it thus provides a basis for a personal style that truly reflects a writer's preference for a form of thought.

Finally, a note has been made of the concordance of singular and plural in English, as well as of the sequential relations between head nouns and their verbs.

EXERCISES

The study of grammar holds an important advantage over studies of many other subjects. Provided the study is pragmatic and empirical, a grammatical hypothesis can be made so short-lived as to be nonexistent, when its proof is demonstrated by the very language used to express the hypothesis. The hypothesis becomes a simple statement of fact, such as we have seen repeatedly with respect to the applications of function words.

However, this same advantage tends to become a liability for the person who desires to improve skills in the use of grammar. Those skills apply to the articulation of thoughts, but an articulated thought comes into existence through the very words one uses to shape it, so that it is difficult to separate a wordless thought for practicing grammatical expression. One of the advantages observed with SPRI has been the extent to which SPRI composition improves one's grammar. When we gain control over our thoughts, we appear to intuitively arrange our thoughts into patterns that we more easily express in terms of grammar. Although this tends to aid our prose, it also encourages us to skip over our grammatical weak spots.

Consequently, some sort of exercise is absolutely essential for developing writing skill, particularly when using SPRI, and particularly at the level of grammar discussed in this chapter. There comes a time when reading and thinking about writing must be cut off and replaced with practice. Ideally, you should begin practicing under some form of guidance that serves to emphasize the principles you have learned, but this assumes you should be provided with some form of thought to put into words.

Fortunately, a novel form of inarticulated thoughts needing expression in English words has presented itself over the past few years as the translation of text books from French to English. Translation proceeds in two steps: (1) literal translation from French to English; and (2) editing and adapting the literal translation. This procedure has made possible some interesting observations. French thinking is definitely different from English, as demonstrated by technical applications that must bring equivalent results. Usually, the differences require just enough change in the thought to make the second step of the two-step translation procedure a precise exercise in grammatical constructions of the sort covered in this chapter.

Accordingly, you will find below a history of the petroleum industry and petrochemical industries that has been excerpted from French texts and translated to the literal English equivalent. Your exercise is to transpose these texts into fluent, idiomatic American English, reorganizing and adjusting the thought as you find necessary. A sample transposition of these same texts is given under "Exercises: Examples" in the back.

Refining is a heavy industry whose characteristics are more conventional and for which the economy is rather close to that of other industries. However, it only gives a slight upgrading of the product that it treats. Indeed, if one ton of crude oil delivered to the refinery is worth 100, for example, the selling price without taxes of the products extracted from this ton after treatment will hardly go over 110 before distribution costs.

The margin of the refiner is thus proportionately weak and lacks flexibility for the selling prices are often fixed by the government. Petroleum companies will therefore be large, integrated and their subsidiaries will be spread around the whole world.

Thus it is that in classifying large companies, done each year by *Fortune* magazine, one finds four oil companies among the first ten world enterprises and twelve within the first fifty. The eight principal international companies represented in 1973 nearly 70% of worldwide production, 60% as the refining and more than 60% of the marketing (outside the communist world.)

The petroleum industry was born in the United States at a time when it was possible for the great trusts to develop practically without constraints. The creation of the Standard Oil Co. by John Davidson Rockefeller (1839–1937) is a typical example of the development of the oil trusts. Rockefeller looked for what could be the bottlenecks of this budding industry and he saw that the products, needing to be refined before being sold, it was necessary to monopolize the refining industry and to obtain the minimum costs for transporting the crude oil. Thus in 1890 he founded the Standard Oil Company of Ohio which, thanks to preferential transportation tariffs, was able to absorb the small refiners by selling at particularly low prices. Ever since 1875 Rockefeller controls a fifth of American refineries and his company benefits from a new boom when in 1979 shipping by pipeline appears which permits lowering the cost of stocking for large refineries even more.

The method used by J. D. Rockefeller for dominating the petroleum industry was thus founded on controlling the economic bottlenecks and on the total absorption of the competitors. Henri Deterding on the other hand followed a very different method to arrive at the same end and to put Royal Dutch Shell on an international plane. While J. D. Rockefeller operated essentially on a local market: the United States, Deterding very quickly understood that he could dominate the other markets only by the "straight line" method, that is to say by supplying a given market from a source of crude that was as close as possible. He tried to have at his disposal a rather large number of zones of production, that were well distributed around the entire world, depending on the probable market. He was helped by circumstances because he acted at the beginning of the twentieth century, that is at a time when isolated zones of production appeared in underdeveloped countries, zones that were easy to control (Dutch East Indies, Mexico, Venezuela, Persia...). For the simple economic reasons coming from the great overall cost of transporting at that time, the corresponding markets fell by themselves under the domination of companies of his group. In addition let's remember that H. Deterding sought always to associate himself with the companies that could exist locally rather than to absorb them.

Another important difference between J. D. Rockefeller and H. Deterding is seen in their relationship with their governments. For J. D. Rockefeller the government was an obstacle since to his eyes it consisted of a fiscal constraint and a legal constraint stemming from the Sherman Act. For H. Deterding, it was a diplomatic, moral and even financial support. Within these attitudes, there was the seed of the current great problems in the relationships between companies and the governments of the large consumer countries.

From this date on, autumn of 1913, international oil lost its exclusively private character. Even for the American companies, the influence of the United States government appears after 1920 and is strongly regulated in 1943 by the report of the Committee of Foreign Affairs in the Senate.

After 1918, other large companies, Texas, Gulf, Cities, Sun, Phillips appear in the United States as a result of the Sherman Act, but especially from the expansion of the worldwide market. In addition, the center of gravity of this market was displaced from lamp oil (kerosene) to gasoline, thus was transformed which facilitated the coming of newcomers. It is a matter here of a phenomenon that is essentially economic, for the changes in the market facilitate the entrance of new companies. For Esso, for example, lamp oil represented 44% of its sales and gasoline 15% in 1912. In 1927, gasoline went to 41% and the sales of lamp oil to 11%.

From the thirties on, the preponderance of the principal international companies of today in the worldwide oil market was established. They were an essential part of the hydrocarbon industry which explains the fact that integration, concentration and cooperation are academic traits of the petroleum industry.

This concentration and this cooperation which could be called agreement or cartel corresponds to a need for economic organization. One could say that pure competition is a favorable factor in manufacture and distribution, but that it is harmful in the exploitation of natural resources. In fact, it encourages waste at the expense of future generations, it makes it difficult to have stability in the raw material markets and it prevents having the necessary very heavy investments that require a long-term guarantee, in spite of the self-regulation created by the market itself.

After the Second World War, the center of gravity of the market was displaced once again, but this time from gasoline toward fuels. In addition, for reasons of economic security, some consuming countries encouraged the development of new national companies. It is the same in the producing countries who sought to better control a key industry for their development. These three phenomena favored the entrance into a difficult market of a new series of companies, because of the size of the competitors already there.

What then can be defined as the principal characteristic of an international oil company?
Without doubt the first is the integration from exploring up to distributing. In addition to the value of distributing the risks of production over a wider industrial activity, the absence of a single link in the industrial chain renders the company vulnerable to external economic actions which would be recuperated over the ensemble of its activities.

The second corresponds to the diversity and the quality of its crude oil resources. Its supply should be worldwide according to the idea of Deterding, and it should include the large zones such as the Near East, Venezuela and Africa.

The third corresponds to the diversity and extent of the market for finished products. A worldwide geographic base is not enough. It is also necessary to have a wide range of production of which petrochemistry should be a part, after gasoline and fuel.

The fourth refers to the idea of minimum economic size not only for the whole world but especially for each geographic zone where it is installed and, in the interior of each of these zones, for each phase of the industry.

Finally, it should be added the notion of a trade name on a worldwide scale, an international symbol creating a reflex of confidence in the consumer. Therein lies a very important task the great complexity of which often escapes the non-specialist. The psychological significance, the color of the trade mark for instance, must be favorable for all areas of the world, in spite of mentalities and reactions that are often in opposition. The costs of research, publicity and change in service stations are always very high. In order to transform the network of Esso, Humble and Enco into Exxon, it took up to 100 million of dollars for the United States alone.

Concerning the choice of raw materials, there were two distinct directions to take in the 1960s. It was conventional then to show that the United States had built their petrochemical development on ethane; indeed, the exploitation of great natural gas fields that were necessary for satisfying their energy needs furnished under good economic conditions a by-product, ethane, that was well adapted to the manufacture of ethylene.

On the contrary, Europe and Japan, countries who had natural gas fields that were not great, had based their petrochemistry on naphtha, then considered a by-product from refining crude oil. At that time the demand for heavy fractions of oil and principally heavy fuel for the production of electricity, left available large quantities of naphtha that did not find sufficient outlets in the manufacturing of motor fuels. Thus the price of naphtha was close to that of a fuel $18/t in April 1971. It is thanks to this favorable economic situation that the European and Japanese petrochemical industry saw a spectacular development, not only where the derivatives of ethylene were concerned, but also those of propylene, butadiene, and benzene, coproducts of naphtha steam cracking. This situation had as a consequence a rapid increase in the consumption of petrochemical products, so much so that from the year 1972 and the beginning of 1973 naphtha became a product so sought after that one saw a definite increase in its price: $42/t in April 1972 on the Rotterdam market and $56/t in July 1973. The petroleum crisis at the end of 1973 amplified this phenomenon; the cost of naphtha passed rapidly to $130/t at the end of 1974; today it reaches $240/t.

This situation had led the petrochemical industry to look for other raw materials that would be better adapted economically to the needs of the market. Thus a tendency has been observed since 1971 toward using heavier fractions from petroleum refining, such as atmospheric gas oil and even heavy gas oil. More recently, following better recovery of the associated gases in the oil fields of the Near East and those of the condensable gases in the gas fields (North Sea, Indonesia) the European and Japanese petrochemical industry oriented itself toward using propane-butane, often mixed with naphtha and even ethane for countries bordering the North Sea. But since the availability and cost of these new raw materials, gas oil as well as gas from liquified petroleum, could be uncertain and susceptible to related variations, one saw the development of flexible steam crackers capable of treating different raw materials in the same unit that the operator chose depending on the cost and needs of the units downstream. Finally, the tendency of oil and gas producing countries to integrate themselves more and more toward the downstream, by manufacturing more complicated products had the consequence of construction of new installations producing ethylene by cracking ethane and manufacture of methanol from associated gases, in the Near East in particular.

Since the capacities of these plants surpass by far the local needs, their products profiting from a cheap raw material market, are able to compete with the manufacture of the industrial countries.

The markets in the world were very profoundly disturbed during the period 1971–1984 by the economic recession and by the evolving rise in costs of production, following consecutively the increase in the price of petroleum raw materials.

This increase in costs affected the great intermediary markets particularly in underdeveloped countries. Indeed, it was felt in the '60s that the low cost of petrochemical derivatives, fertilizers and polymers, principally would have to be a decisive element in the industrial growth of these countries by the end of the century. The precautions made at this time are far from having to be accomplished. First of all the reason can be attributed to the weight of the cost of the raw material in the final cost of the product; it represents today 85% of the operating cost of a steam cracker, while in 1972 it amounted to only 48%. Then, for the same period the investments were multiplied by 4 times in current currency and by 1.6 in constant currency. Because of this, the petrochemical derivatives have lost part of their cheapness able to be widely distributed for these countries.

In the industrialized countries, the economic crisis had the consequence of slowing down consumption, such that the capacities of production remain very much in excess in relation to the needs, which weighs heavily on the financial equilibrium of companies.[2]

5

AN AUDIENCE FOR YOUR PROSE

INTRODUCTION TO CHAPTER 5: THE PAY IS THE PRESTIGE

In the descriptions of SPRI experiments, under "Verbal Tools: Classes of Thought" in Chapter 1, there is a sentence which reads, "These were serious, commercially effective articles, which could in no way be restricted by their parallel purpose of experimenting with the classification of thought." Subsequently Chapters 2, 3, and 4 concentrate on composition and writing; and aside from mentions of reader surveys and general acceptance, there is no discussion of the effects produced by the articles. However, it is appropriate to ask about those effects. Did the articles make their authors famous and rich? Was the price of company stock influenced by them? What was the effect of the articles on the acceptance of specific technology? When did an article sell a multimillion dollar plant? Did an article ever produce the desirable effects of an advertising campaign? Without answers to such questions, the shrewd reader would reject this book as having little use for enhancing or advancing a professional career.

It so happens that answers to many of these questions came all at once, with the sense of discovery of a new concept, and accompanied by answers to secondary questions such as how and why.

While the classes of thought were still being articulated through publication of the experimental articles, M. W. Kellogg Company was developing a new process for the manufacture of ammonia, which is the single most important synthetic chemical. Since it was not clear which parts of the new process would be covered by patents, and which by proprietary know-how, the Kellogg people were secretive about the process. On the other hand, publicity about technical achievements was a means for selling Kellogg's engineering services. As a result, the company did publicize its ammonia technology, but in bits and pieces. One time, the subject would be the optimum pressure for generating hydrogen by methane reforming, another the yields and conversions in the ammonia synthesis reaction, and still another the mechanical design of pressure vessels.

From my point of view, such articles afforded good tests for experimenting with the substitution of thoughts in a frame article, because many thoughts were repeated in subsequent articles under a different guise and a different emphasis. In addition to my experimental articles, articles on ammonia appeared in other magazines and society papers under the bylines of Kellogg engineers, and still other articles were written by reporters working for other technical magazines. At one point during the time span of this accumulating editorial material, the entire industry fell into acceptance of the new ammonia process like a tall tottering tower. Consequently, the time required for commercial acceptance was phenomenally short—shorter than the time for commercial acceptance of copying machines or bottling machines, or front wheel drive, for example. M. W. Kellogg sold $300 million of the new plants before it was even able to get the first of those plants built.

This means, obviously, that the people who authorized those expenditures had to be sold on an idea that as yet had no physical embodiment. Although not so obvious, it also meant that the idea had been promulgated by publications in the technical journals. Some sales engineers claim that they can sell an ammonia plant person-to-person, but an experienced designer knows that the necessary explanations can not be made that easily. Moreover, Kellogg engineers who sold the plants say that they did not attempt lengthy technical explanations.

But what, specifically, could have made those articles about the ammonia process so effective? We have a partial answer from chapter 2: *concepts*. Somehow, the accumulated editorial material had promulgated a concept that represented Kellogg's process. To help find an explanation, Tom White, who was the public relations man for Kellogg, provided me with copies of all those articles that had been published. A number of these did develop a distinct concept; and even though the actual ammonia process had yet to be revealed, it became possible to arrange the individual concepts of those articles into a pattern that reflected the process. Each concept was given a label and identified with a problem that it solved. Then all the concepts were reviewed to discover which would create a problem solved by one or more of the other concepts.

Eventually all the concepts were related by lines representing problems answered or solved. The resulting diagram was fascinating. Not only did it relate the published articles, but it also revealed the process and the pattern through which that process had gained such wide acceptance. It now became time to test not only the diagram, but also my understanding of the process, the assumptions of some articles as articles of concept development, the questions asked and answered by the concepts, and the concepts themselves.

Tom E. O'Hare had been influential in process design and development at M. W. Kellogg. He was also a friend of many years. I invited him to lunch at Le Chambertin on West 46th Street in New York. As soon as we had finished with the menus, I took out of my briefcase a sheet of paper on which I had made my diagram, and laid it in front of him. Tom leaned over to study it, while I watched without daring to speak. Whatever I expected, I was not prepared for what followed.

He jabbed a finger at the paper, "That's me!" he exclaimed. Then he leaned closer. "That's..." and he named an engineer. "And that's..." another one. He kept on until he had named four engineers, and then paused. Again, jabbing a finger, he said, "And that's all of us!"

Rarely are so many questions answered so effectively and so succinctly. Tom had accepted the diagram without a thought. He had accepted the notion of a concept, as concept, by claiming it as his own idea. He had promptly (and generously) identified other concepts with the engineers who had generated them. He had revealed the true spirit of a research and development team, which he pointed to a key concept and said, "That's all of us." He had confirmed my understanding of the ammonia process by accepting the arrangement of concepts. Because all the concepts had been discovered independently in published articles, he had confirmed those articles as articles of concept development. And because the accumulated editorial material containing those articles was the only public source of information about the process, he had indicated that editorial material as the means by which the process had been promulgated so rapidly—by which $300 million of plants were sold before the first one could be built.

The more than twenty years which have intervened since that luncheon have seen still more effects of those articles. Its ammonia process has been a mainstay for M. W. Kellogg. Other companies that designed and built compressors, turbines, heat exchangers, and so on, in conformity with the Kellogg concepts have fared better than their competitors. Technical innovations implicit in the concepts have been adopted in other aspects of industry. And the original M. W. Kellogg engineers, particularly those identified by the publications, have been much sought after throughout the industry. Many of them now hold top positions elsewhere.

Although much of this would not have occurred without a viable process and qualified people, neither would it have occurred without the effects of the editorial material. Industry is replete with innovations that have not realized their potential because the concepts of those innovations were not published. The effects on M. W. Kellogg's ammonia process can be taken as typical of the effects of a published article of concept development. They show the payment that one can hope for from publishing.

This payment can be summarized in one word: *prestige*. The shrewd professional should know in advance how to make use of such prestige; otherwise the effort of publishing is wasted. Also, the shrewd professional should approach publications like a design problem, seeking an optimum among the possible choices. What kind of publication carries the most prestige, and how is this achieved?

The questions will be explored by, first, discussing methods for evaluating the professional journals ("Reading Between the Pages"). Many professional people have come to identify with one or more journals that serve their profession. Sometimes these journals offer the format for a prestigious article, frequently not. In any event, an author who judges professional journals subjectively in terms of his or her own reading is making a mistake.

After discovering how to find the most prestigious journal, the writing professional may come to feel that his or her material does not belong in a magazine at all. There are books; and we will compare the advantages of publishing in a magazine with those of publishing in a book under "Betting on Books."

In either case, the publishing writer will need to deal with editors, who can have a drastic effect on the publication for better or worse. So we shall next consider "Editors and Editing." Finally, we shall consider, from the author's point of view, the one profession that tries to make the bridge between writing and publication: public relations.

READING BETWEEN THE PAGES

This section feeds back to "Procedure for Prose Composition" in Chapter 2, where the first of four criteria was presented as establishing a subject, an audience interested in that subject, and a reason for that interest. Reference was made to professional journals and the Audit Bureau of Circulation, in order to qualify an audience according to its function. That identity by function with the identity by profession pinpoint the audience like two intersecting straight lines fix a point in space.

Writers who have successfully fulfilled that first criterion are now ready to seek a professional journal that addresses their identified audience. Since there are about four thousand professional journals, the possibilities are so varied that one can best use a checklist of considerations such as the following:

Title

Affiliations to professional societies

Circulation

Issues per year

Contributed articles per issue

Authors' biographies

Articles published to fit a theme

The title of a journal can usually serve to identify the field of professional interest.

An affiliation with a professional society not only identifies the journal with the society but also suggests that the journal may be read only by society members, that the circulation is that of the society membership, that the published articles comprise mostly papers delivered at society meetings, and that the articles fit arbitrary society themes, such as clean air, energy conservation, AIDS testing, and so forth.

A journal's circulation should be determined, because a larger number of readers lends more prestige to an article.

The number of issues per year bears on the remembered impressions of a journal and its articles. Various studies have shown that one month between issues is near the optimum for keeping the contents fresh in readers' minds. If the publishing period is longer, readers are slower to make associations with the published ideas; if the period is shorter, any one given idea gets too much competition. A variant of this notion of remembered impressions applies directly to the choice of a journal to carry a specific article. Experience shows that original and esoteric subjects tend to be overlooked, particularly by technical audiences, who need to know the structure into which the ideas fit. Consequently an author should seek out articles related to his or her own article, note relations and differences, and seek publication in the same places.

A similar type of optimum also exists for number of articles per issue of a journal. The tendency is for journals to carry a number of articles on different subjects in order to interest a variety of readers. However, too many varied articles tend toward confusion. The optimum seems to provide variety without preventing the individual reader from finding what interests him or her. In poor times, with fewer advertisements and consequently fewer editorial pages, some journals try to maintain their editorial diversity by publishing the optimum seven to nine articles, but with each of those articles condensed to the point where it has lost its usefulness.

An authors' biography identifies both the individual and the source of the information. Some journals, which identify an author with a few lines at the end of the article, tend to confuse staff writers with contributors; and this sort of confusion tends to reduce the prestige of the article. Also, if an article represents years of experience of a professional team, this can be made apparent in a biography.

Finally, an author should take note of a journal's tendency to present themes related by term or general subject rather than by concept. These are useful to the journal because they can be used to sell advertising and to simplify editorial decisions; but they can dilute the effect of an article; and they tend to conceal an article that does not fit the theme.

This foregoing checklist of concerns represents almost an archetypical subject for library research; and if a trained professional has been able to prepare an article without becoming familiar with library research, now is the time to make the introduction. Without a doubt, researching one's subject is the single most important activity prior to publishing in a professional journal. If this text has skimmed over such research, it is because of the assumption that you are a beginning writer who has non-verbalized thought, based on years of professional training, to serve as the information for your first few articles. However, you will quickly exhaust your training, and you should be prepared to start researching at the first suggestion of any doubt.

Some people may think they have exhausted their capacity to contribute to their profession, when they find it necessary to search out already documented information to round out an article. That attitude represents a misconception, which was revealed to me through working with consultants. Although work as a technical reporter had involved continual research amounting to three to four hours for every hour spent writing, research of that sort was not necessary when I became an editor dealing with articles written and researched by others. Nevertheless, the background of information built up through research was useful for editing, and I tried to replace the previous direct involvement in research with a vicarious involvement obtained by aiding different consultants who had become business friends over the years. McGraw-

Hill maintained an excellent business library for its employees and advertisers, and I gave those consultants access to that library. I was repaid with an excellent education, because the consultants were top flight experts with astronomical hourly rates that they had to justify by extreme efficiency in their research.

Once a consultant asked me to help him discover what we could about typewriters. The information available at McGraw-Hill was amazing; but I could not help wondering why this consultant was doing a report on typewriters. He wasn't, he explained. He was doing a report on ABS plastics (acrylonitrile-butadiene-styrene), and an important projected market for ABS plastics was typewriter cases. Contemplating that response, it became clear that here was a man who charged well over $100 per hour for rummaging through published material. He certainly could not collect those fees for his skills in sorting through the publications; our excellent librarian did that for him. The basis for his fees was the questions he asked.

We saw, under "Applied Problems" in Chapter 2 of this book, how a pertinent problem gave significance to Dr. Alex Oblad's research organization. Now, in the presence of this consultant, it was possible to see two sides to one of New York City's better business libraries. On the one hand, there were shelves full of published information, anywhere from six months to thirty years old, and of little interest to many of the McGraw-Hill editors because it was already published and was not new. On the other hand, there were revered answers to past questions, classified and organized, and waiting for those gifted people who might be able to lend those revered answers new life through new questions. Standing beside that consultant, as we respectfully described our problem to the librarian, I felt like Ali Baba at the moment of intoning "Open, Sesame."

With that concept in mind, we can run through an exercise in researching. You have been given a check list of questions about professional journals and a description of purpose for each of those questions. If your curiosity ends there, you are at fault. It is essential for your success in communicating that you be sensitive to the presence of problems. Those six questions, for example, merely suggest the larger problem of how to discover those professional journals whose answers to the questions best suit you; and that brings us back to the problem of how to do research.

We begin with libraries. You have available to you three different types: company libraries, university libraries, and public libraries. The company library will be available to you only if you work for the company. A university library should be open to the public, if the university is partly supported by grants or public funds. Public libraries are available to the public. However, whatever library you choose to start with, your admission will be tempered by the way you present yourself. Experience with hundreds of research projects has demonstrated that it is best to think in terms of an admission ticket; and that ticket is your research problem. Think the problem over, carefully, then write it out on a piece of paper that you will carry with you. The effect that a carefully articulated problem has on a trained librarian is truly amazing. So, here's your ticket:

I am doing a study of professional journals serving the field of (your field). If feasible, I would like to list all such journals, as far as the total number and perhaps the individual titles. Once I've determined the total, I would like to screen the list according to circulation, frequency of publication, and whether they publish articles by professionals in (your field). From this screening, I would like to select no more than twelve journals. Subsequently, I would like to screen individual copies of those twelve journals according to their content, in order to select no more than four journals that can be recommended as publishers for articles in the field of (your field).

Resolving the problems associated with this statement will require considerable time and effort. You should consider that as an investment. If you do your research properly, you will bring away a packet of information that is unavailable from any other source and will be useful to you for as long as you write for publication.

Note that much of your problem-statement could be replaced by an inquiry after the four best journals for publishing your articles. Since *best* is ambiguous, like *good*, it needs a qualifier; and your qualifier is the selection procedure implicit in your statement.

Armed with your statement, you go to the most convenient library. Depending on that library, you may be referred to another library, perhaps after a telephone call or a reference to an interlibrary publication. If so, be sure to note the details about the library to which you are referred. If it means a trip, telephone or write beforehand. When you arrive, still armed with your problem-statement, your first step should be a summary presented in some sort of encyclopedic reference to professional journals (e.g., *Directory of Publishing Opportunities in Journals and Periodicals*, published by Marquis Academic Media; *Guide to Scientific Periodicals* by M. J. Fowler; *Scientific and Engineering Literature*, published by Libraries Unlimited).

When approaching one of these directories, first determine the point of view of those who prepared the directory, in order to learn how to best interpret the information, and to get ideas. Viewed at this stage of a research project, any individual problem can be seen as another way of classifying the available information. Many lucrative publications are merely generally available information reorganized for the convenience of a specific group of people. Contemplating this with your professional training, you are likely to arrive at unique insights for other classifications suited to problems shared by people with your background.

Next, expect to sort out for further screening a dozen journals chosen according to the checklist of questions. Be sure to organize the names and features of the journals chosen for further screening, because the next step of your study will be a confusing one. In some library, which you may need to travel to, a substantial portion of the selected journals will be displayed usually alphabetically with one hundred to two hundred other journals in a reference room. Each of those one hundred to two hundred other journals will compete visually and intellectually for your attention so stridently that the decisions of your first-step screening are apt to become confused and lost. You will be tempted to come up with a new selected dozen, but remember that your previous decisions were made in the abstract according to recorded statistics and are therefore more reliable.

Once you have located the journals, your study should include at least four copies of each journal. At this point, evaluation becomes more subjective, and your dominating question becomes whether you would want your name and your article to appear in such a publication. Again, any judgments and observations should be put into notes for the appropriate journal, along with the foregoing six questions.

The next step is to get some idea of what a journal's readers are like, through determining what advertisers feel about those readers. On the one hand, the author of a contributed article is in much the same position as an advertiser. Both solicit the reader's attention; both hope to involve the reader; and both hope that the involved reader will act. On the other hand, the author solicits publication by the journal, whereas the journal solicits paid advertisements from advertisers. There are sometimes complicated techniques through which a journal offers detailed analyses of its subscribers to advertisers. Although these analyses are not made available to contributors, the contributor can study recent issues of the journal to see what its advertisers think. Here is what to look for:

Volume of advertising

Type of advertising

Content of the ads, with respect to
—type of product offered
—manner in which the product is sold
—cost of product

The volume of advertising can be determined simply from noting the number of pages in the journal. Postal regulations and other rules tend to fix the ratio of pages of advertising to pages of editorial material for each of the various segments of professional publications. A journal published by a museum or lay society may carry 40 percent of its space as advertising, whereas a journal published by a trade or profession may carry 60 percent of its space as advertising. The price per page for advertising in a trade journal with sixty thousand subscribers may run around $5,000. A successful journal might have one hundred to one hundred and fifty pages, so that the gross receipts for that journal might be (60 × $5,000) = $300,000, or (90 × $5,000) = $450,000. This compares to subscriptions income that might run about (60,000 × $1.50) = $90,000.

After volume, the next most noticeable aspect of the advertisements is whether they are classified, one-column, two-column, half-page, full-page, black-and-white, or color. This does not reveal much of direct importance to an author, except for the relative leverage of the profession characterized by the ratio of investment in production facilities for the individual worker. The professions of some industries are responsible for the design, construction, and operation of installations costing millions of dollars, whereas other professions in other industries may have higher personal incomes but hold responsibilities for little valuable material. This difference is readily apparent in the journals serving the different professions. The ones responsible for expensive installations may find themselves confronted by page after page of full-color ads, whereas those without such responsibilities may find the pages of their journals rather drab.

Within the general environment established by the volume and color of the ads, it becomes necessary to study content to decide how advertisers characterize the journal's readers. The three questions—type of product, its sales procedure, and its cost—are asked together of each ad, as one pages through the journal. For example, some journals carry many pages of ads for employment opportunities. Although an author might sympathize with this, it is doubtful that an article will have been prepared for professionals seeking a job. Other journals carry many pages of ads offering engineering services, indicating that designers expect the journal to be read by executives with the authority to award engineering contracts. Such journals might be optimum for exposing some types of novel technology.

In like manner, ads can also indicate sales and costs. For example, a full-page ad in color might offer new technology for the design of a manufacturing facility, and include the photo, telephone number, and address of a salesman familiar with the technology, while a typed ad might offer consulting services, also with a telephone number and address. Obviously, sales and costs resulting from the two ads will be different. Other differences make the advertisers' perceptions of the readers even more apparent. For example, two journals, which could both handle the same subject and which both carry mostly contributed articles by academic people, carry different ads as indicated by the table below. This comparison shows that the advertisers regard the left-hand journal's readers as impulsive individuals, while the readers of the right-hand journal are regarded as professional representatives of design and construction firms.

Volume of advertising	40 pages	60 pages
Type of advertising	cars, collectibles, books, tours, drugs, telescopes, cameras, exercise machines, whisky, classifieds	outdoor furniture for parks and gardens, building materials, plumbing, books, nursery stock, seeds, fertilizers, electrical equipment, park maintenance machinery, instruments
Manner of sales	direct mail orders, retail	through wholesalers' catalogues, mail order
Cost of product	$50–15,000	$5,000–500,000

With such comparisons, an author can get a good idea about which journals would publish an article, and who might be reading those journals. Professional services are done for profit. If a publication serves a profession, that publication should also expect reimbursement from the profit-taking professionals. However, most professional groups have been reluctant to pay their publications directly, whether as subscription costs or as dues to a society that supports the publication. The pragmatic solution to this problem has been to find a third party willing to pay the publishing costs. This third party comprises all those merchants and manufacturers who have products and services to sell to the members of the profession. If a profession is commercially active and consumes large quantities of products and services, it attracts many suppliers who readily support the publications serving the profession. Because of the support, the publications carry more information useful to the profession. This enables the profession to be more progressive and more profitable, and to consume more products and services, which attracts more suppliers who give more support to the publications serving the profession.

The intermediate means through which suppliers support a publication is advertising. Advertising specialists need to know who reads which periodicals and for what reason. An author needs similar knowledge. Advertisers employ various services to get their knowledge. An author can avoid the expense and time for such services by reading the ads. Consequently, this discussion of how to select a publisher among the professional journals has used an analysis of advertising. The analysis assumes that an author wants to reach an optimum number of interested, influential readers who can understand what the author is writing about. It may be, however, that this analysis has made all journals less appealing. Books offer an alternative. However, book publishing should be considered thoroughly before rejecting the journals.

BETTING ON BOOKS

In Chapter 2, under "Thought Patterns Applied in Design," it was noted that prose composition naturally progresses through stages, each of which takes all that went before as the situation for its unique problem, resolution, and information. Accordingly, SPRI is suitable for use in books. However, the treatment of some subjects lends itself to one or more magazine articles but not to books, and vice versa. For example, the same principles of ammonia technology, as described in the introduction to this chapter, have also been presented in Strelzoff's *The Technology and Manufacture of Ammonia*. Although the book used the same principles of SPRI composition as did some of the articles, it necessarily assumed a different reason for reader interest and did not build a conceptual structure like the articles.

When should an author use one or more articles, and when should that author turn to a book? The answer depends too much on the author's motives, the accessibility of a suitable journal or book publisher, and the nature of the subject to allow for generalizations. Instead, book publishing will be described briefly and compared with journal publishing.

The effects of organizing a book's contents can be illustrated using two books cited previously: *The Structure of English*, by C. C. Fries, and *The Reader Over Your Shoulder: A Handbook for Writers of English Prose*, by Robert Graves and Alan Hodge. Both of these books are monumental in their accomplishments. Both are recommended for anyone who wants to write English well. We will first consider the one less known, in order to see how its acceptance was affected by its organization.

The Structure of English separates good from bad grammar quite simply; good grammar is easily understood, and bad grammar is not. As described earlier, Fries's description of English is based on fifty hours of taped telephone conversations from Ann Arbor, Michigan. He analyzed that conversation as if he were cracking an unknown code, and thus approached English without the usual biases. Moreover, his techniques were orthodox; he was president of the American Teachers of English, and head of the linguistics department at a university. Many of his principles were incorporated into books for teaching English to indigenous speakers of Spanish and other foreign languages. *The Structure of English*, then, appears to be an attempt to extend the understanding of English beyond the narrow limits of scientific linguistics.

However, despite these conditions, which should have made this book widely read and widely accepted, it appears that Fries's efforts have been hampered by the very background that allowed him to produce the book—pedagogy. Teachers are notoriously bad teachers, because they teach to a captive audience over which they exert absolute authority in terms of grades. This authority is enhanced and reinforced by an educational system that demands absolute obedience through requirements for awards and acceptances; these awards and acceptances grow progressively more limited as they grow more advanced. In order to achieve a professional career, a student must learn to commit to memory whatever the professor has prescribed, otherwise the student fails exams and falls by the way.

We see the way pedagogy would promulgate a novel idea when we turn to *The Structure of English*. There, a useful idea (an empirical approach to spontaneous language) is carried through with disciplined, scientific rigor. However, the results are presented in the manner prescribed by pedagogy. The reader is given a description of the experimental method, and then the results of the method in the form of lists to be committed to memory. Only when readers come to the last two chapters, "Immediate Constituents" and "Practical Applications," do they find any suggestion of the actual problems that Fries's scientific achievements can be used to solve. It is in "Immediate Constituents" that the reader discovers the two descriptions of baseball referred to in Chapter 3 of this book. And in Chapter 4, we saw how Fries's lists can be used to resolve important practical problems that appear when we have a preordained system of thought; we need signals, and Fries shows us how we can find those signals among relatively few words. Moreover, these are only a few of the many problems whose answers are found in Fries's lists. A computer software designer should be able to make a livelihood from Fries's book. Unfortunately, most of those practical problems have yet to be articulated.

Like Fries, Graves and Hodge performed a scientifically rigorous empirical experiment and reported the results in a book. Their experiment involved reading extensively and noting whenever their reading was interrupted by an awkward expression. It is important for this experiment that there are two authors. One could have been idiosyncratic, but not two. After noting many awkwardnesses, they found that these were not limited to newspapers and hastily written pieces, but also appeared in the writing of some of the most renowned philosophers, scientists, and writers of their time. By organizing all their discovered awkwardnesses, and presenting the organized results in book form, Graves and Hodge have done something to improve what they consider a crisis in the general quality of English. They divide their book into three parts: a history of English; a description of the experiment and the results; and many paragraphs that they analyze and correct with paragraphs of clean copy. In effect, these three parts conform to an SPRI organization. The history of English presents the situation out of which arises the problem of generally poor contemporary writing. The resolution then becomes the discovered awkwardnesses of expression, which are tracked down by reading and cataloguing.

There are thirty-six awkwardnesses, characterized by poor punctuation, which lead Graves and Hodge to offer the best concise description of English punctuation to be found anywhere. Finally, the thought class of information is provided in the analyses of the sample paragraphs. A reader can convert these examples into exercises by reading the originals and their analyses without the clean copy, and then composing his or her own clean copy. Since the corrected authors include Bertrand Russell, Ernest Hemingway, Julian Huxley, C.E.M. Joad, and Aldous Huxley, among others, this exercise also exposes the student to better-than-average thinking.

This book may be taken as another example of book composition. Look at the table of contents to see what is attempted. The whole book is organized around the assumption that professionally trained people have non-verbalized thoughts worth publishing. It starts with examples of non-verbal thoughts and proceeds through a succession of problems related to organizing thought for publication, giving the organized thoughts graceful expression, writing clearly, choosing a medium of publication, and getting published.

If the chosen form of publication is to be a journal, the author may never see the original manuscript again, but instead get for approval an edited copy or galleys. If the publication is to be a book, its author will see the text again, and again, and again, before the book is printed and bound. Book authors usually take a more active part than article authors in preparing their texts for publication—so much so that it sometimes seems that the book author functions as part of a publisher's staff. Because of this, an author's performance can have pronounced effects on the cost of publishing a book; and publishers usually provide explicit instructions, impose rules, and extract penalties for breaking the rules. Generally, a book's author is expected to do the following:

1. Prepare the manuscript in a specified form.
2. Prepare the illustrations in a specified form.
3. Review and make final changes in the original manuscript after it has been marked up by a copy editor.
4. Review galley proofs and make corrections but no changes.
5. Review page proofs for layout, locations of captions, etc.
6. Prepare the index.

Physical specifications for the manuscript usually prescribe the paper as 8½" × 11", 20-pound bond, which will accept pencil marks. The side margins are usually 1¼", with 1¼" at the top and 1" at the bottom, in order to make room for corrections and printing instructions. The type should be clean, dark, and preferably in an elite font. This allows one to make an accurate estimate of the page surface covered by the text when printed in another style of type.

The requirement by most book publishers that an author either provide or pay for camera-ready illustrations is for many authors the strongest deterrent to writing a book. Unless the author has available the services of a drafting room, the illustrations will cost about $40 each. A typical technical book with 300 pages will bring on costs of about $6,000 for preparing its camera-ready charts, graphs, and illustrations. An author who is asked to provide such costs by a journal should look for another journal.

Once the manuscript and camera-ready copy have been accepted by a book publisher, they will be reviewed by a copy editor and corrected for spelling and so on, and then transferred to a production editor, who will add printer's instructions. All these are added as marginal notes. The manuscript bearing these notes is then returned to the author. Although extreme changes at this stage imply that an author is unsure and perhaps not capable, the author is theoretically allowed unrestricted changes, including entire manuscript pages. The approved manuscript is then returned to the editor, who forwards it to the printer, who sets it in type and prints a set of galley proofs.

Because galley proofs are the first time that an author sees the text in print, he or she may not be able to resist making changes on them. Book publishers do allow this, but usually charge for all changes affecting more than 15 percent of the lines. More important, the galleys afford an author the chance to review the type and arrangements used for headings, subheadings, lists set in type, italicized words, and so on. While visual rather than thematic, many of these things do act as punctuation, and anything that might be confusing should be discussed with the book's editor.

Approved galley proofs and camera-ready illustrations are next marked with instructions for page layout and sent to a compositor, who will lay out the pages. In order for the compositor to locate the different illustrations next to their place of reference in the text, each must carry a number and be referred to by that number in the text. This is the author's responsibility. Also, many of the charts may be reduced, so the author should note, either on the edge of the camera-ready illustration or the margin of the galleys, those charts that will be used for calculations. Such a chart is usually marked "working chart." Because the cost of publishing a book is directly proportional to the number of pages, publishers like to reduce illustrations to a minimum size.

Some months after galley proofs are returned, the author will receive a set of page proofs. This will be the first time the text appears as it will in the bound book. The author should check the illustrations, their captions, and their textual references, in order to see that all match as they should. If they do not, or if the layout is confusing, this should be discussed with the production editor. Considerable expense and perhaps the compositor's contract may be involved. Also at this point, the pages will for the first time be numbered, so that the author can prepare an index. Both the author's pride in the book and his or her respect for the reader will be revealed by the index; any professional who uses books knows that indexes are important.

Indexes can be easily prepared using the following process: (1) mark the page proofs; (2) put the indexed words and page numbers on cards; (3) alphabetize the cards; and (4) type the index from the alphabetized cards. When marking the pages, skim the text and underline the sentinel words. Much time can be saved later if one skims the pages ahead for repeated references to an underlined sentinel word and writes those page numbers in the margin of the page on which the sentinel word first appears. Type the cards. Alphabetize. Type the index. The entire chore should take less than thirty hours; and it gives an author the opportunity to read his or her text one more time.

With the index, the author's duties are finished. The book should appear in about three months. All in all, the delay between the time a manuscript is first sent to a book publisher and the date of publication is about one year. The corresponding delay for an article to appear in a magazine (called "lead time") is about six weeks. Book publishers usually pay royalties annually or semiannually; and one year is a reasonable time to estimate for writing a book. Consequently, it takes two and one half to three years after starting the manuscript for an author to receive payment for a book on a professional subject. For this reason, many book publishers are willing to pay an advance based on the estimated sales of the book.

EDITORS AND EDITING

We began this chapter with an incident showing how a group of published articles had a dramatic effect on the acceptance of ammonia technology, on the commercial success of a company, and on the careers of the people who wrote the articles. Condensed into one word, that effect was described as *prestige*. Prestige was suggested as the purpose for publishing in professional journals; and authors have been warned that they should know how to use prestige if they want to benefit from publication. However, that was the first time that this purpose entered into the discussions of this book on how to write and publish. In Chapter 1, we saw that professional people often pursue entire careers during which their progress in thinking is separate from their language, and that this alienates them. We also noted that many studies show that language offers a discrete environment within which a person can adventure to realize his or her nature. If the purposes implicit in such statements are now tested against the activities set forth in this chapter, we see that such purposes do not serve. We have shifted our stance, moved from one attitude to another, put our command of English to new use.

If we consider the notion of prestige, we see that, rather than coming from a direct person-to-person exchange, prestige depends on third parties. A co-professional may benefit from an article that you write, and may value you and that article for that reason. However, this relation with a co-professional will not bring you the benefit of prestige until others enter the situation. In the terms of information theorists, your article may have contained "conditional" information related directly to the subject of the article, but to achieve prestige that article also needs "contingent" information from an association with variables introduced by other people. Practically, this means that the carefully crafted article discussed in Chapters 2, 3, and 4 can not of itself achieve prestige and there is no use in going back to revise that article, because prestige can not serve as the primary purpose for an article, but must come as a by-product. The very title of this book addresses professional people who also write, rather than professional writers; and we have from the beginning been approaching this point, which is an impasse. Thoughtful writing, no matter how brilliant, can not achieve the commercial goals implicit in publishing.

This impasse has spawned the four thousand or so professional journals of today. Thousands of professional people write. Those thousands reach a stage beyond which their writings can not win the recognition they seek. So, like a river flowing around an obstruction, those writers change direction, enter a new stream bed, and turn their articles over to the editors of professional journals. These journals and their editors in turn act like bankers whose currency is information. They borrow information from their authors, and like modern bankers, repackage it into various sorts of mutual funds, each suited for an audience to whom the fund is rented. Like money, the information is of practical value only when it has a use made possible through know-how. In the packaging process, the journals create prestige, which enhances their value to subscribers and advertisers, and which the journals share with their authors.

However, this analogy also brings out a common weakness—responsibility. Just as an investment manager is responsible for the composition of a loan portfolio, so an editor is responsible for the contents of a journal. Some journals try to avoid this with a statement that "responsibility for the contents rests on the authors..." but such a claim means nothing, because the one positive way to avoid responsibility is not to not publish that article. Other reactions to responsibility encompass virtually all the problems that a publishing professional may have with the editors that handle his or her manuscript. Those editors not only select an article from among others for publication, but they also delete or modify parts of that article. The possibilities for this are so broad that generalizations for even one profession are impractical. The best that one can do is to keep the purpose firmly in mind and keep alert to the editor's fear of responsibility. Generally, this fear will exhibit itself as an aversion for originality and clear articulation; and the editor's solution is euphemism. If you say that tests "prove" something, for example, the editor may say that the tests "indicate the possibility of." Unfortunately, this same precision that makes an SPRI text better for a reader may make that text disturbing to an editor.

However, journals and their editors usually know best. To illustrate, I have had articles with nearly identical contents appear in a scholarly journal with a circulation of about five hundred and in a large trade journal with a circulation of over seventy thousand. The version in the scholarly journal was untouched by editing; and the trade journal version was edited almost beyond recognition and made distastefully simple. There has been no response to the scholarly publication; the response to the trade journal has included hundreds of inquiries and numerous references.

Editors tend to use euphemisms for their own titles, as well as for difficult ideas in a text. A glossary of some of the euphemistic editorial titles you might find in journal mastheads are the following:

Glossary of Masthead Titles

Publisher	Owner or owner's representative
Editorial committee, editorial advisors	Well-known professional people who have made themselves

	available to the journal's editors for consultation, and who may attend a meeting with the editors four times per year
Editor-in-Chief	Editorial manager
Editor	One who may review manuscripts, edit manuscripts, write articles, and attend editorial meetings. A journal is heavily edited if it has one editor for every two articles per month
Contributing editor	Writer
Copy editor	One who edits all material to be published, always for grammar, sometimes for grammar and style
Managing editor	One who oversees the assemblage of individual issues of the journal
Art director, presentation editor	One who prepares or supervises preparation of illustrations, arranges text and illustrations on pages, and arranges ads and editorial material in the journal
Editorial assistant, administrative assistant	Secretary

However we decide to name it, prestigious publication is associated with editing; and editing is sure to bring problems for the trained professional who begins, as this book advises, by learning to put nonverbal thoughts into words. Fortunately for some, there is one profession that is devoted to solving just that sort of problem—public relations.

PUBLIC RELATIONS

There may be some sort of poetic justice in the fact that public relations, a profession devoted to explaining things, should be so misunderstood. Although many public relations specialists promote themselves as marketing experts, journal editors tend to identify public relations people as those who can provide an interview with the right person, and company executives tend to regard their company's public relations people as those who can put them in touch with the right editors. Because all of these perceptions are true, many people fail to understand the function of public relations people, and thus fail to exploit a valuable resource. Add to the foregoing perceptions some typical incidents.

Incident 1. I was doing a report on energy, in which I planned to feature various types of equipment and to show how to use the equipment through charts.[1] The plan was to have the charts drawn to my specifications by leading manufacturers, each of whom was more than willing to provide them. However, I had in mind a novel application for steam turbines, and the engineer assigned to prepare that chart tried to persuade me to abandon my request and substitute a more conventional application. The discussion lasted longer than I would have thought possible. Finally, despairing and getting irritated at the engineer's air of superiority, I was preparing to leave, when in walked the company's public relations man. Within a few minutes we were in agreement. The chart was prepared and published.

Incident 2. An unusual amount of interest had been generated by a short article drawn from a paper presented at a meeting of cost engineers. The original paper had been the result of a hypothetical analysis that four young cost engineers from different companies carried out as a group in their spare time. I met with them, and we decided that I might be able to identify study subjects that could be used for more articles; and they would do the necessary studies. It seemed like a good arrangement, of benefit to both the engineers and the magazine. We were all in agreement and enthusiastic; but although we met four times, we somehow were unable to get down to specifics. I have always felt that our project failed for lack of a public relations person.

Incident 3. After seeing the manner in which one group of random articles had by chance complemented each other to promulgate M. W. Kellogg's ammonia process, I began to wonder if such a program could be carried out deliberately. I explained my theories to a high-ranking public relations man for a large corporation. He took my ideas, put them into a report, and persuaded the corporation's management to test the theories using a series of articles published in various magazines over the period of a year. I suggested that the article carrying the key concept be carried by the journal I worked for, and I wrote that article for the signature of one of the company's engineers. To my embarrassment, that article was rejected by my managing editor. It was only when the company's retained consulting public relations man explained the article, that the managing editor agreed to accept it.

These three incidents provide enough data to create a useful concept of public relations. That concept is *contingency*. The role of public relations people is to provide a contingent perception. Test this concept against the incidents.

In incident 1, the engineer and I had reached an impasse. I do not know why. Perhaps it was not even technical. Perhaps it was because I, an outsider, was presuming to ask him to do something he knew about. On the other hand, neither do I know how we came to agree so well with the public relations man present. Whatever he did, it was contingent to the basic technical discussion. We did not air any part of that discussion before him, but the chart he got us to agree on was acceptable to both the engineer and me.

In incident 2, the group of editor and four cost engineers seemed to have everything in its favor. The previous paper had showed the relative effects on the profits of a hypothetical chemical plant for variations in investment costs, feedstock costs, and price. (Surprisingly, a 10 percent increase in price is worth a 100 percent increase in investment.) It seemed that there was a world of similar questions to be revealed with similar independent studies. But nothing that I could suggest satisfied the engineers, and vice versa. I'm sure that a public relations person would have been able to bring us into accord.

Finally, incident 3 best reveals the truly contingent nature of public relations. One might well ask why a large corporation, with a staff of salaried public relations people, bothers to retain a public relations consultant. Answer: For contingent opinions. The corporation's public relations staff might be able to advise an executive, but they are too much a part of the corporation to express a credible, objective opinion of an article to an editor. Incident 3 made the need for a contingent viewpoint even clearer, when the managing editor called me in for an opinion. Unable to frame an impersonal objective comment, I had to excuse myself. Similar situations have confronted me, when I wrote press releases for professional friends, and then had editor friends ask me for an opinion of the press release. You are likely to experience a similar reaction if asked for an objective opinion of an article that you have written.

With contingent opinions as the concept through which we see public relations people, we are ready for their help. But first, we should know a few things about them.

It is essential that a public relations person have easy access, on familiar terms, with all the top executives of a company. Also, for the same reasons, the public relations person should be privy to all information about the company. This easy access to executives and information may give some staff public relations people an inflated air of importance; and it may cause them to appear aloof, particularly to professional people in middle management. However, good public relations people are self-effacing and accessible. Furthermore, professional people, particularly technical professionals, are a source of the sort of information much needed by public relations people.

There are discrete fields of public relations. The field for your company may be that of your profession. If so, you are fortunate (see chapter 6). On the other hand, the public relations person for your company may devote his or her time to social publicity for the company executives in their own communities. If you do not know the field of effort of your company's public relations, look at its ads and note where they appear.

Many companies have one person who handles both advertising and public relations. In such cases, there is a tendency to pay more attention to the advertising, because it involves an impressive budget and authority. On the other hand, public relations—articles—is not only less expensive, it is more effective. If you can combine professional knowledge, writing skill, and a cooperative disposition, you can be extremely valuable to your company's public relations person.

In some cases, where engineers were assigned to write articles and charged the writing time the same as their engineering time, those articles were astronomically expensive—much more expensive than advertising. This is probably true for most professions; and public relations people know this, so do not ever imply that you want to write on company time.

Finally, never submit an article for publication without first clearing it with your company's public relations person. If you can not get that person's help, at least get his or her agreement in principle.

Before taking up the publishing process, the options available in the journals should be reviewed to make sure that, like a good designer, you can offer your thoughts to a publisher because of choice and not because of necessity. This chapter has focused on obtaining the highest prestige from an article, which assumes an aggressive attitude toward publishing. There are certainly many trained professionals who pursue careers because they enjoy them rather than solely for money or prestige. Such people might prefer to sacrifice some of the prestige of publishing in a well-known journal with large circulation for publishing in a more relaxed, social atmosphere. There are two possibilities for this: anonymous publication through association with technical editors and reporters, and publication in the smaller journals.

If you live near the editorial offices of a journal that serves your professional field or related fields, if you are in a position to possess authoritative understanding in your field, if your performance can benefit from knowing the most possible about contemporary activities in your profession, if you enjoy professional gossip, and if you enjoy or benefit from seeing your ideas anonymously exposed in a publication and watching the effects, then you might consider association with a technical editor or reporter. If you do comply with all these qualifiers, the odds tilt toward your being in some sort of sales, but you could also be a highly specialized professional in an esoteric field. A condensed summary of conversations that occurred with Phil, a catalyst salesman, and Dan, a process design engineer, will show the symbiotic relationships that can exist between a reporter and those two extremes.

Dan is one of the world's three or four leading designers of plants to manufacture a widely used basic chemical. There are over three hundred such plants in the United States alone, and Dan has been responsible for a substantial portion of them. However, a conversation with him does not give the impression of concentrated knowledge so much as a relaxed, almost lazy attitude, along with a youthful enthusiasm and gullible naivete. Although Dan may have written articles about his field, he has been too lazy, he says, and he has preferred to tell two or three reporters things that could be published as anonymous technical news.

Phil was the sole salesman for a catalyst company's line of extremely expensive catalysts used in the manufacture of various chemicals. Much more intense than Dan, Phil did write articles. Although he traveled constantly and was continually in communication with all sorts of people who used his catalysts, he felt he could not know too much about current technical activities; and he made a point of calling on me from time to time, just to talk.

One day, after working hard together on an article, Phil and I relaxed to gossip. Phil, complaining, began to tell of the difficulties of his job. Suppose, for example, a chemical manufacturing company decided to build a new plant. That company would get in touch with three or four engineering companies, and ask them for an estimate for the plant. Each of those engineering companies would, in turn, get in touch with Phil for information about a catalyst to go with their design, which would be slightly different from the others. Also, two catalyst manufacturers competed with Phil. This all meant that, for one plant, three catalyst manufacturers would each be preparing special information for each of four engineering companies. Although much of this prepared information was the same, some of it was significantly different. Furthermore, as he called on each of the engineering companies, Phil was required to study the designs that would use his catalyst, and in this way, he saw all four competitive designs during development. There were millions of dollars at stake on the bids, so Phil had to be extremely careful about how much he revealed to whom. Most irritating to him were some of the poorer designers who tried to trick him into revealing information about the others.

The manufacture Phil talked about was Dan's specialty, and I could not help blurting out, "How about Dan?"

Off guard, Phil caught his breath, then laughed. (There is something about Dan that leads one to smile at the mention of him.) "Oh, him!" Phil said, "Dan knows everything."

Not long afterwards, Dan told me about a new device that had been installed by a manufacturing company to reduce air pollution. It seemed like worthwhile news; it meant that one plant among hundreds was not polluting. However, I felt morally obliged to discover from Dan how many people could know what he had just told me, and to point out that, if the information were published, Dan could be identified as the source, through process of elimination. There might be some other way to get the news out, if he preferred. But Dan shrugged and opined that the polluters should feel the pressure. I published the story, and a few months later, Dan told me that more of the antipollution devices had been installed.

You, as a trained professional, might be like Phil, or Dan, or somewhere in between. Wherever, you may be able to enjoy seeing your ideas appear anonymously in published print. However, you should exercise care in the choice of the reporter with whom you associate. There are two extremes. On the one hand, many reporters regard as their property every bit of information they receive by whatever means; at the opposite extreme are reporters who regard all received information as a loan, until released either by the person who gave it or by events that make the information redundant. Usually these two extremes will each declare his or her policy, but if they do not, they are easily identified. The reporter who respects no confidences will depend on interviews for information, take notes, and may even carry a dictating machine. By contrast, the reporter who treats confidences as loans will have researched your subject to the point where he or she can carry on a knowledgeable conversion about the subject without ever bringing a pencil into view. You should know, however, that such reporters are seeking confirmation for guesses or interpretations that they have made; and you are likely to give them much information through such confirmations, nonchalantly, without being aware of it. If the reporter is honest, he or she will tell you what you have revealed. Also, such a reporter should be able to tell you about unpublished details of recent events.

The other means for a more social and less prestigious publication exists among hundreds of small professional journals that carry little or no advertising and have circulations of one thousand or less. In these journals, the functions of publisher, managing editor, and editor are often combined in one person, who may be a practicing or retired professional who publishes the journal as a hobby. Associations with such people can usually be rewarding, open, and relaxed.

The best way to get acquainted with small journal editors or technical reporters is through something you have read in their publications. Make sure you know things related to the subject, and telephone or write the person through the journal. Tell what you want to know or to talk about; and let them understand that you have nothing to propose. Ask for permission to visit them at their office; or invite them to lunch. If they avoid you, do not persist. If you do become acquainted with some reporters or editors, your association will benefit, if you know something about their work. This is discussed in the next chapter.

6

AN OFFER THEY CAN NOT REFUSE

INTRODUCTION TO CHAPTER 6: AN IDEAL SITUATION

Imagine that you are an employee of a manufacturing company. The price of the company's product depends on its quality, and that quality is dependent on the technology in which you are trained. Applying this technology is a staff function, rather than an operating line function, and you are a member of a small staff with a group vice president for your boss.

Having learned about thought and language, you have become intrigued with the problems of writing about your technology, and have written some essays about various aspects of your work. You have been able to show some of your writing to your boss, in order to get an authoritative opinion of your writing. You make it clear that you are not interested in becoming a writer, but that you are curious to see if writing can help your command of the technology. Your boss is sympathetic, so that you can ask him to suggest subjects for you to write about.

The company employs a staff public relations woman, who visits your boss and your staff group from time to time. During one of these visits, you ask her for a second opinion on one of your pieces. During the discussion, you explain your purpose for writing and describe how the writing has affected your command of the technology. This description leads to the question of whether or not writing about the subject makes you know more, about what reading your pieces does for a technical colleague, about how much your pieces tell outsiders, and about how much of the company's know-how is shared by similar companies with similar staff groups. The conclusion is that reading most of your pieces serves to educate only contingent groups, such as your company's customers. You reach the conclusion that the competition knows it already, so why not educate the customers. With that line of reasoning, the public relations woman decides that a series of articles from the company would have great promotional value. She decides to get the feelings of your boss and the top management on this idea, and you tell her you would be willing to take on a writing project, in your spare time, with your boss signing the articles with you to show he has reviewed them for non-disclosure of any proprietary technology. The boss and the management are sympathetic, your boss discusses the arrangement with them, and you are ready to begin.

However, the public relations woman asks you to wait a bit. She calls the managing editor of a preferred journal and arranges to see him for lunch with a staff editor who is familiar with the company's technology. During this lunch she tells the two editors about the recent clearances she has been able to obtain. She asks the editors which subjects hold highest interest for the company's customers, and which subjects are of most interest to the magazine. The specialist editor says the magazine has already covered the company's technology in recent articles. But the managing editor suggests there might be other things. The public relations woman invites the editors to visit the company to discuss the possibilities. The company will pick up the tab for transportation, lunch, and so on.

Back in the company's offices, the public relations woman uses the few days before the editors' visit to bring you copies of the journal with the articles mentioned by the specialist editor, and discusses those articles with you. You feel that the articles are accurate but superficial. She leads you into discussing related subjects. Your growing familiarity with conceptual thinking inspires you to identify each of the published articles with a concept peripheral to the central purpose of the technology; and as you try to explain this, you get the idea of a diagram and use that to explain the overall technical purposes of the group to which you belong. She likes this and asks you to have the diagram formally drawn up. This you do.

On the day of the editors' visit, you see them going into your boss's office with the public relations woman. A few minutes later, you are called in. You find copies of your diagram are distributed over the table, around which the others are seated. You are asked to explain. You do, sticking to problems and their resolutions. As you talk, you realize that you are being made to appear as the expert. You politely withdraw when you've finished your explanation. An hour later, the group stops by your office to thank you.

Later, the public relations woman and your boss stop by to say that the journal has agreed to accept a series of three articles signed by you and your boss. Your boss half-heartedly suggests that you might take some writing time from your regular work, but you decline, asking him only to reserve the offer in the event you get behind in your deadlines. You ask the public relations woman if she would be willing to look over each of the articles. She readily accepts; and your boss approves that arrangement.

You write the articles. The public relations woman reviews them with you, and delivers the edited versions to the journal. They are published. The reception is overwhelming. The company increases its profits. Your boss takes his company stock options and retires to Florida. You are promoted to his position. The public relations woman quits, starts her own company, is fabulously successful, and is elected woman of the year. And everyone lives happily ever after.

Now, this fictional sequence reveals two things. First, there are a number of steps that must be taken to obtain the publication of any article. Second, there are a number of qualifying situations that aid the successful publication of an article.

The necessary steps are:

1. You must write.
2. You must produce some evidence of authority for the subject.
3. The idea of your article must be reviewed by the journal.
4. The article must be scheduled for publication.
5. The article must be edited.

The qualifying situations are as follows.

You are an employee. Publicity about your function can affect company profits. You have a boss who has authority in the company and is sympathetic to writing and publishing. Your company has a skilled public relations person.

There is a prestigious journal devoted to your profession. Because your profession affects your company's profits, your company is now or is potentially an advertiser in that journal. The editors of that journal have enough confidence in their authority to be able to schedule articles in advance by subject.

You have studied writing and practice writing. You share your thoughts and seek opinions about writing in general. You keep separate your job performance and your practice of writing. You can separate writing about your profession from the practice of your profession.

Chances are that this optimum combination of situations occurs only rarely. Although there are many companies with a public relations staff, the individuals on that staff are not often as skilled and hardworking as the woman in the example. The odds seem about even that a supervisor will be as amenable as the one in the example. Many professions exert only a contingent effect on the company's product, so that the company has no interest in publicity related to the professions. However, most professions are served by at least three professional journals, so that the editors may actually compete for good articles. The most important feature of the example is the author, who can write, discuss writing, keep separate the job and the writing, invent, explain, be self-effacing, combine patience with persistence, and keep things in perspective. An ability to write is only one of the abilities affecting successful publication. However, none of the other qualities are too difficult to achieve, so that they can be assumed for the present discussion.

Keeping in mind the five steps required for publication, we shall first consider how editors go about their work, in order to see how the necessary steps impinge on editorial activities. Next, we shall address the situation of the professional employee whose function does not affect the company's product, and who thus can not expect company support in efforts toward publishing. Finally, we shall consider some of the problems of modifying or adapting a given article to suit a journal. Although descriptions of actual incidents may seem discursive, they do connote and suggest contingencies, and actual incidents will be used to demonstrate many of the points.

EDITORIAL PROCESSES

A typical editor normally performs the following functions, listed in order of their decreasing time demands:

1. Edit scheduled articles.
2. Review and correct galleys and page proofs of the journal.
3. Specify, review, and correct the art associated with articles.
4. Review and approve or reject unsolicited articles.
5. Deal with authors and their representatives.
6. Maintain records of correspondence, as well as of articles submitted, rejected, edited, and published.

7. Aid in planning article subjects for succeeding issues.
8. Represent the journal on request for purposes of publicity and public relations.
9. Find authors willing to provide desired articles.
10. Schedule specific articles of a given length for upcoming issues of the journal.

Before considering the way that these functions affect editors, consider the following incident. In the mid–1970s, a large California oil company developed a problem in the operation of one of its refineries, so that it could not produce enough gasoline to satisfy its customers and had to buy gasoline from its competitors. The company was going to lose something like $70 million over the course of some months. The California newspapers appeared delighted with the development, reporting it as if telling of a political scandal. The New York magazine for which I worked had a San Francisco correspondent who seemed to share the attitude of the local newspapers; and he sent us arm-long teletype messages about engineering errors, lines at gas stations, and so forth. Some editors on the New York staff brought the teletypes to an editorial meeting and proposed a major article on the refiner's difficulties. However, two things cast doubts. There was little technical explanation in the teletype; and the nature of refining is such that major failures take months or years to develop. It could be that some technical journals had already reported on this story, and if they had, our journal would look foolish with late, non-technical coverage. The editorial meeting evolved into an argument about whether or not to go ahead with the story. Finally, the managing editor gave me a few days in which to discover any reasons for not doing it. If I failed, the others would proceed.

That was a problem. A quick teletype brought no help from the San Francisco correspondent, who wanted to do the story. Since there are at least five journals covering that field, it would be necessary to review back issues of all five for a thorough search. Instead, I telephoned a friend who was a senior refining editor for a competitive journal.

"Dave?" I began, and started to ramble about what the California newspapers were saying.

"Oh," Dave interrupted me, "I've given those guys such a hard time, I thought I'd lay off them for a while."

When I revealed my ignorance, he explained. Three senior design engineers working for the California refiner had evolved a new approach to the design of thick steel walls for high pressure vessels. Three years previously, they had presented this approach at a meeting of the American Petroleum Institute. They had applied the approach to a hydrocracking vessel for a new refinery being built by their company.

If the approach worked, it would benefit the entire industry. Unfortunately and surprisingly, careful examinations made during startup of the new hydrocracker revealed that a crack was developing inside the steel wall. The operating pressure had to be reduced, which reduced the throughput and gasoline production. My friend Dave had visited the plant, seen the vessel and radiographs of the crack, and had published those radiograph pictures in his magazine. We on the New York journal dropped our plans for an article on the subject.

Now, that incident is typical of behind-the-scenes editorial activity. Considered against the necessary activities of journal editing, it all comes under item 7; and it shows that actions meaning much to a journal's public image actually take a small percentage of the editor's time. In fact, those activities consuming most of the editor's time (items 1, 2, and 3) actually have a negligible effect on the journal's content. Of course, subscribers like journals to be easy to read, with no printing errors, and well-illustrated, but what counts most is the subject matter, which is resolved in activities 4, 5, 7, and 9. Surprisingly, perhaps, most editors begrudge the little time given to those activities, because it is so little as to seem unimportant.

Also, consider the California refiner's relation to publishing in the technical journals. Because that refiner sells gasoline, it does not get direct benefit from articles published by its professional employees. However, in the incident, the previously published technical papers might have won sympathy among related professions; and if the newspapers' technical editors had been more capable the API papers might have avoided adverse publicity. Otherwise, this incident shows typical relations between any one professional journal and other publications. Editors of professional journals tend to read competitive journals, as well as newspapers and news magazines; and those editors tend to be influenced by what they read. Usually, they will avoid a subject they've seen in a competitive journal, but will be attracted to subjects aired by lay publications with large circulations.

Thus an author who wants to be able to influence editors should read widely and learn to use his or her profession to interpret the news.

Returning to the list of editorial activities, it can be seen that those activities through which articles are accepted are 4, 7, and 9. First consider activity 4, reviewing and approving or rejecting unsolicited articles. Although that activity may account for 30 percent of a typical journal's editorial material, my advice is to abandon it. Unsolicited articles are reviewed by groups of editors, any one of whom can usually reject them. Such articles have no advance explanation, so that any amount of originality makes the subject unfamiliar, and conventionality makes the subject hackneyed. When in doubt, it is always easier for an anonymous editor to say "no." Unfortunately, it does not work to place a blind telephone call to a managing editor, who may tell you to send the article in, because that article will be treated as an unsolicited article.

That leaves activities 7 and 9, planning article subjects and finding authors to cover those subjects. Note that these were the activities carried out by the public relations woman in the idealized sequence of events. Moreover, she was smart enough to go to the managing editor. She knew that, except for the journal's department editors, the managing editor worries most about keeping the magazine well-supplied with good articles. On the other hand, the managing editor tends to be the busiest, so she did not waste his time; she only went to see him when she knew she had something; and she saw him over lunch (for which she paid).

Chances are, you will not have such a skilled public relations person to aid you. But if you are employed by a company that does have a public relations person, you should be sure to make the acquaintance of that person, in order to discover the role that he or she prefers to play in getting you published. In case you are either an independent consultant or both your supervisor and your company's public relations person have no interest in what you publish (beyond clearing the final draft), you are on your own so far as the journal is concerned.

ON YOUR OWN

In order to see how you stand, compare the list of five steps necessary to publishing with the list of ten editorial activities. You have two alternatives. You might try to somehow accomplish steps 2, 3, 4, and 5 in conjunction with activities 7, 9, and 10, in which case you could delay writing your article until you had a journal committed to it. Or you could go ahead and write your article in the hopes that your clear and thoughtful prose will win publication through editorial activity 4, as an unsolicited manuscript. This book begins with the first alternative.

You need to somehow persuade an editor to plan your article's publication in a future issue (activity 7), to let the editor see you as an author willing to provide that article (activity 9), and to satisfy the editor's schedule (activity 10). In order to successfully share in these activities, you will need to establish yourself as an authority (step 2), get the idea of your article considered by the editors (step 3), get an editor to schedule your article (step 4), write that article according to expectations (step 4), and get your article edited (step 5).

In one incident, an author managed to accomplish all these things seemingly at once and with ease. Bill identified me as the Plant Notebóok editor and sent me an article with a nomograph. I wrote to tell him that I found his write-up of the necessary calculation excellent, but the nomograph simplistic. Bill telephoned to explain that he was superintendent of operations at a large plant in Texas; and that he usually tossed his copy of our journal on the general table in the operators' room. He liked composing nomographs of practical use to his operators, and he liked seeing the journal lying open to the Plant Notebook section on the table, and perhaps with one of his nomographs published there.

He had me hooked. Although plant operators were an educational step below the audience targeted by our journal, I could not resist the image of the journal lying open to my section amid the clutter on the table of a busy operating room. I not only published the nomographs that Bill composed for his own operators, but also sought his advice about other articles.

This incident not only illustrates how the author-editor activities may be combined, but it also reveals a back road to frequent publication, a journal's departments. Sometimes a department editor may have long backlogs of accepted articles awaiting publication; more often he or she is a little worried about where the article-after-next is going to come from. Most important, a department editor alone decides what is acceptable and what is rejectable, so that there is no anonymous editor to take the easy way out with a "no." The problem becomes that of compatible subject matter. Frequently a journal published in your field of interest will have departments devoted to related subjects from other fields. Sometimes, you may be able to solve this problem in journals outside your immediate field. For example, as editor of *Chemical Engineering*'s Materials Engineering Forum, I published many articles by mechanical engineers and metallurgists, who would normally subscribe to and publish in other journals.

Another method for introducing yourself to an editor is to telephone the journal and ask to speak with the editor who handled a certain article. In "SPRI and Design Thinking" in Chapter 2, an article is discussed on designing brick-lined reactors, with a suggestion as to how SPRI thinking exposed a fundamental design principle. Some years after that article, a man called to talk about the use of brick linings in a highly corrosive environment where scrap plastic was chemically dissolved for making vinyl chloride. Although the man did not disclose the process, I recognized it as new and controversial, and was interested. He later caught my complete attention by telling me I had a stereotyped concept of process design procedures. That led to a series of interesting conversations lasting over six months. Although that caller was not interested in publishing, I pleaded with him for various articles, and would have interceded in favor of almost anything he submitted for general review.

Still another alternative to submitting an unsolicited manuscript is the letter of inquiry, which if handled correctly, can win the attention of an editor with a minimum of effort. The trick lies in saying enough to establish your authority and create interest, without presenting a definite basis on which an idea can be rejected. This can usually be accomplished through inquiries about published articles. However, the inquiries should be composed so that the editor will feel the need to answer you him/herself, and not simply route your letter to the author. For example, you might see a common link between several articles by different authors, and write an inquiry about that link. Or you might write first to the author.

Give nothing but the facts, but make sure to include all the necessary ones. The letter should contain your business address, an address to the editorial department, the purpose of the letter, the reason for the letter, an explanation, and your title, as in the following example.

Giant Products Co.
1000 Research Retreat
Technology, NJ 07039

Editorial Department
Journal of Catalytic Discoveries
1100 Sixth Avenue
New York, NY 10020

Purpose of this letter: To reach editors who might be knowledgeable about the following articles: The Eutectic Points of H_3PO_4 Solutions, *Journal of Catalytic Discoveries, 50,* June 2, 1987; Fluorine as a Coagulant, *Journal of Catalytic Discoveries, 49,* Sept. 12, 1986; and Gypsum Acid Equilibria, *Journal of Catalytic Discoveries, 50,* Jan. 24, 1987.

Reason for this letter: To discover articles or other means of information exchange related to this field.

Explanation: Giant Products Co. has for years used phosphoric acid catalysts in systems related to those of the above articles. We feel that this is a wide field of interest, so that additional articles would be of mutual benefit. I would like to discover, from the appropriate editor, if your journal has more articles on this subject, and/or if you might be planning such articles.

Thank you for your time.

Henry J. Writer
Research and Development Dept.

This letter has been composed to accommodate the mail-handling methods typical of journals. The sources of letters, press releases, brochures, and so on, usually delivered twice a day and addressed to the editor-in-chief or the managing editor, are sorted by secretaries, who decide according to subject which editor should see each piece of mail. If the envelope bears the name of an individual editor, it usually goes to that person without being opened. If the inside address bears the name of the editor-in-chief or the managing editor, that may be enough to have the letter routed to that person. Because secretaries can not know all the areas of interest of all editors, because of the sensational appearances of most press releases, and because most editors can not be counted on to reroute mail for which they feel only marginal interest, mail sorting and distribution is one of the weakest points in a journal's information-handling system. For example, news editors readily admit that their magazines normally use less than 20 percent of the press releases they receive, and that there may be much news of value in the discarded releases. Some of the best SPRI news stories were literally scavenged out of the secretary's waste basket.

Without a personal address, your letter of inquiry may be little better than throwing pennies in a barrel. Thus, another feature of the blind letter of inquiry should be reproducibility. Compose the letter so that it can be photocopied and the signed photocopies repeated, even to the same journal. In the sample letter, for example, the internal address could be blank for typing in on a photocopy. If yours is a busy field, there may be as many as six possible journals to which you might send three to four letters. Publishers send out inquiries in this form, and usually do not mind receiving them.

The blind letter of inquiry does hold an advantage over a letter to an editor whom you know only marginally. Editors vary enormously; and one area of great variation is the attitude toward letters of inquiry and unsolicited manuscripts. Whereas one editor may be indifferent to the point of rudeness, another may go so far as to help you rephrase your inquiry to help you meet the needs of some other editor. As part of the SPRI experiments, I edited entire articles by friends and acquaintances, and instructed them to resubmit the edited articles. Some of those rejected and resubmitted articles were accepted by editors who seemed not to recognize them, although they had rejected them earlier. By the same token, do not jump to conclusions about an editor or a journal, when you receive no response. I still remember a young engineer who sent an enthusiastic letter of inquiry about an article. I was on vacation, and my answer was delayed; whereupon the young engineer wrote a nasty letter to the editor-in-chief about our deceitfulness. When I got back, I answered the letter of inquiry, but did not give further help.

In sum, the best approach is through activities 7, 9, and 10. Identify a sympathetic editor in a department concerned with your field of interest, and develop your article along the lines discussed with that editor. Barring that, you may want to go ahead and write the article, on the basis that you obtain experience in writing, even if the article is rejected. In either event, the article should be composed according to Chapters 2, 3, and 4 of this book.

Importantly, the unsolicited manuscript should be accompanied by a cover letter that can sell the idea of the article without one's reading the manuscript. It is remarkable how much such cover letters, rather than the manuscripts they present, can dominate the subjects of discussion in an editorial meeting. Your cover letter should include the following points: the subject of your article, the specific audience interested in the article, the reason for the audience's interest, recent and forthcoming events related to the subject, the significance of the events, and the trends involved. To illustrate, let's again take up the design of brick-lined reactors mentioned in "SPRI and Design Thinking" in Chapter 2.

Giant Products Co.
1000 Research Retreat
Technology, NJ 07039

Editorial Department
Journal of Catalytic Discoveries
1100 Sixth Avenue
New York, NY 10020

The enclosed manuscript might almost be regarded as a sequel to "Designing Brick-Lined Reactors," which appeared in your journal seven years ago (*Jour. Cat. Dis.*, 43, May 17, 1980, pp. 143–157). The field of linings has seen new developments (intimately associated with broad catalytic applications) that suggest some updating of that earlier article.

Specifically, all industries disposing of plastic wastes or otherwise carrying out corrosive, catalytic high-temperature reactions are interested in the modern innovations related to ceramic linings. There has been a group of new amorphous ceramics introduced for such linings, and as you know, the problem of plastic wastes continues to get larger.

As explained in your previously published article, the problem of ceramic linings comes from the different rates of expansion between the ceramic lining and the vessel's steel shell, as the vessel is heated from the temperature of lining application to operating temperature. However, several companies are proposing a new technique, which while simple in concept promises radical improvements. These linings, which are amorphous, rather than aggregate like bricks, can be applied hot to a hot steel shell, rather than laid in by hand at ambient temperatures. Thus by choosing the proper application temperature the lining can be designed to have at ambient conditions of shutdown a stress equal and opposite to the stress at operating temperature, so that both stresses are much lower.

This completely changes the design procedure excellently described in your earlier article. Now there are two unknowns, lining thickness and application temperature, with an optimum combination of the two. Several companies of my acquaintance are now installing these systems; and while the names of those companies are now confidential one or more might be available by the time the enclosed article is published.

I look forward to hearing from you.

Henry J. Writer
Research and Development Department

    An energetic secretary can look up the earlier article referred to in this letter, along with who edited it, and can send this letter to that editor along with a copy of the earlier article.
    There remains another avenue to publication—one that editors do not readily discuss, that does not fit with the ten listed activities, but that often puts a journal's editors in a most vulnerable position so far as accepting manuscripts is concerned. This method usually involves a detour around catering to advertisers.
    Virtually all professional journals will claim with some justification that their editorial judgment is not influenced by their advertisers. However, it so happens that a journal can evolve an image of itself, that this self-evolved image is successfully promoted to advertisers by the advertising space salesmen, and that the journal's editors wind up struggling to perpetuate the image they have created, in order to live up to the claims of those salesmen. Let us assume, by way of illustration, that over a few years the pharmaceutical industry discovers a new family of beneficial drugs. These drugs are complicated, so that their use becomes the subject of a series of articles in a medical journal. The drug makers see that those articles have an enormous effect on prescriptions for the drugs, so the drug makers advertise in that medical journal. However, as the medical profession becomes familiar with the new drugs, there is less need for more articles, whose frequency accordingly drops off to zero. This leaves the medical journal with a lot of ads about drugs, but no articles. The drug makers notice this and wonder if they should advertise elsewhere. That doubt travels fast, until it impinges on the journal's managing editor, who at the next editorial meeting brings up the need for some articles that the salesmen can show to the drug makers as evidence of the journal's continued interest.
    This type of situation is so common that many of the larger journals have regular meetings devoted to article subjects ("image" subjects) and their role in maintaining a journal's image. Oftentimes these im-

age articles become mandatory, and are scheduled and assigned to an editor, even when there is no known author. Surprisingly, the resulting articles are often of high quality. They usually treat a subject in some depth, and are the kind of article that a professional person might clip out and file for future reference.

Usually a journal will try to maintain its image indefinitely, so that the subjects of the image-making articles are scheduled for retreatment every four to five years; and an editor might be assigned such an article a year in advance of its publication. If you are not fixed on a subject, a clever way to find an editor, who might even be ready to help you write, is to go through back issues of your profession's journals, discover three to five-year-old feature articles that suit you, and then telephone the journal's managing editor. Ask him/her if an update is planned for that old feature article; if so, which editor is assigned to the update. With luck, you'll find an editor desperately searching for an author; and if you can carry out this gambit, you may obtain the best possible conditions for publishing.

With a publisher for your article, the next concern is the editing. In many cases, you will be unaware of any editing until your article appears in the journal. In other instances, you will have a copy of the edited version for approval. In either case, reading your edited article is likely to be a disturbing experience, particularly if you have worked hard to perfect your writing. Theoretically, the first four chapters of this book should equip you to deal with the situation. Actually, that will hardly be the case. If you find that the editing has actually damaged your article, a simple statement to that effect is not enough. It may be your article, but it is the editor's journal. The two of you must arrive at a mutually satisfying version. How do you go about this? This difficult question is the subject of the next section.

COMPETING FOR ATTENTION

From the choice of its subject through acceptance for publication, an article is treated individually. Although the author makes choices in the process of composition, there is rarely, if ever, a tendency to write two articles at once. Instead, the author tends to direct the single article toward a purpose and to choose the parts for their intrinsic value toward that purpose. Similarly, review boards and editors tend to evaluate each article individually for its intrinsic value. Rarely, if ever, do editors compare a group of articles for the purpose of selecting only part of that group for publication. Instead, if many good articles make their appearance at the same time, the journal builds a backlog of articles awaiting publication; and although a large backlog may make editors less receptive, each new article is considered separately.

Once accepted, however, all this changes; each article competes with other articles in the journal's schedule, for preferential treatment and for the reader's attention after publication. Many authors wishfully believe that a good article will win the attention it deserves, as long as it is made available. However, experience shows that this happy belief is simply not true. Consequently, the successful author must face the fact of competition between published articles, and must strive to win out in that competition. Competition is tacitly accepted when an author selects the journal best able to publish an article. When an article is accepted by a journal, its author surrenders control, so much of the means for competing for the readers' attention must be anticipated and provided for before the article is accepted. Accordingly, some aspects of what follows should be considered feedback to earlier sections, and what is discussed here should be written into the article.

First, consider how the journal handles the article. Although detailed procedures differ among the thousands of professional journals, a certain sequence of events must take place. Because different aspects of the article assume prominence during one or another of these events, a review of the sequence aids in planning for the events, and even in doing something about them at the time. Acceptance of an article initiates the following:

1. The author is asked to sign a waiver.
2. The article is attached to notes from its review, given some identification, and filed with other articles awaiting publication.
3. The article is selected from the file, assigned to an editor, and scheduled for publication.
4. The article is edited.
5. Illustrations for the articles are assigned to the art department.
6. The edited manuscript is sent to the author for approval.
7. Headlines, decks, and table-of-contents summaries are composed.
8. Any special treatment is decided on and initiated.
9. The text is set in galleys, pages are made up, and lines are added or subtracted.
10. Page proofs are reviewed.
11. Advance tearsheets of the magazine are sent to the editors from the printer, and a number of these are usually sent to the author.
12. The author receives a copy of the journal bearing the article, usually with an honorarium.

Signing the wavier. Many journals require that authors of published material first sign a formal statement relieving the publisher from copyright infringement by the author, as well as to give the publisher rights over subsequent use of the published material. Most journals also copyright every issue, so that with the signed waiver, the published article no longer belongs to the author, except for responsibility for plagiarism. When the author receives the waiver form and notification of acceptance, he or she should telephone the publisher to inquire about the backlog and when publication might be expected.

Filing. By the time an article is filed, it will have received written editorial comment. This is attached to the article; the package is given a folder; and this folder is labeled with the article title and the author's name, and is filed with other articles awaiting publication. Depending on the journal's backlog, this file may represent a waiting period of two to 6 months—long enough for many people to forget what was said about the article during review. Once an article is taken from this file, it requires about ten weeks for the article to appear in a published issue.

Selecting and assigning. Manuscript folders are drawn from the file chronologically and in conjunction with the specific plans for the composition of a forthcoming issue of the journal. If the journal carries a lot of advertising for which it maintains an image, an image-making feature article may be scheduled for a specific issue as long as a year in advance, so as to give salesmen the opportunity to sell the appropriate ads. Any article scheduled to appear in the same issue as the image-making feature will get secondary treatment.

Generally, if an article is long and received highly favorable comments during review, the managing editor will attempt to schedule it for an issue with no image-making feature. That means your article will compete with the other scheduled articles for preferential handling in that issue. The choice for preferential treatment depends on a balance of things such as available photographs, timeliness, thematic content, and individual editorial preferences. A clever author can influence this balance. The first step is to discover from the managing editor or his secretary the date when the manuscript is assigned to the editor.

Editing. This is probably the most careful reading that an article ever gets, because the editor must be thoroughly familiar with it in order to decide what to do. Considering that editors constantly handle one article after another, and that they are in constant association with authors and news sources, the editors are usually well informed, although perhaps not trained in the profession served by the journal. Under the circumstances, the first reading by an editor is the most important time for an article to be able to speak for itself; and if the author has been negligent before this point, there is little that can be done.

Illustrations, headlines, decks, and table-of-contents summaries. The article's editor will be working on these almost simultaneously with editing the article. Many editors find satisfaction in winning preferential treatment for an article they handle, even though that means extra work. If the editor likes an article, there may be much that an author can do to help. However, communication at this point depends on the editor and there is little an author can do, except to telephone an offer of help about a week after the article is assigned.

Author's approval. Editors are too busy to delay any part of their work while awaiting an author's approval. Because editors edit one article after another, changes made in any one article can be considered standard; and extensive changes indicate there was probably something wrong with the article in the first place. If the changes are extensive, the edited article may be different enough to allow the author to write an entirely new article on the same subject, and that would be the best reaction.

Special treatment. On the other hand, if the article is unchanged, or the editor otherwise indicates a favorable reaction, the author might telephone to, first, thank the editor for the work, and second, to offer any possible help. The best form of help is the offer of photographs and the opportunity for the journal's agent to take privileged photographs. If the author works for a company with a public relations representative, that person, if forewarned, can be of help at this point. However, an overly forceful offer of photos might be seen as preempting the authority of the journal's art director.

Galleys. The author of an article for a journal should not expect to see these, which will carry the edited version plus the copy editor's corrections. On some journals, even the editors do not see the galleys, whose primary function is to provide the production and art editors with physical blocks of type for laying out the journal's pages in pasted mock-ups. During this work adjustments are made to avoid such things as locating an incomplete line of type at the bottom of a column, locating a bold-faced type heading at the bottom of a column, locating an incomplete line of type at the top of a column, positioning lists of type so that they are broken confusingly, and so forth. All of these adjustments mean adding a few lines here or subtracting a few lines there. Such changes are hardly ever referred to the author, but are handled by the editor, who typically has become adept with such redundancies.

Page proofs. These are a confirmation of the pasted page mock-ups. Editors may brag about adding a column of copy, or even a whole article, "on page," but this is a crisis performance to be avoided by everyone.

Advance tearsheets. Some of the more affluent journals send their authors up to two dozen tearsheets, while less affluent journals pretend that tearsheets are not available. Many journals offer reprints or tearsheets for sale. If you have seen enough of your published article to be convinced it would be useful as a reprint, you should inquire about reprints as soon as your decision is reached. The journal can order an overrun from the printer as part of the regular issue. Under those circumstances, the reprints might cost $50 to $200 for one hundred to one thousand copies. If you have been lucky enough to write an image-making feature, that article will most likely be overrun for sale and distribution to advertisers, and you as author should be able to get a number of free copies dressed up with a cover from that issue of the journal.

Copy of journal and pay. Even the poorest journals send their authors at least one copy of the issue in which those authors' articles appear. Some journals also send their authors free subscriptions. More affluent journals go so far as to pay from $25 to $100 per page. Because the prestige of a published article is more important, the pay is redundant, the subscription is a nice gesture, and the article-bearing issue is essential.

HINDSIGHT TO THE FORE

What happens when an article is published?

In one instance, the title of the article appeared in a survey periodical listing recent articles and their authors' addresses, with the result that the author received about two hundred postcards from all over the world, each card requesting a reprint without any offer to pay costs of postage or reprinting. In another instance, where the author had described the organization needed for plant design, his engineering friends joked that he wanted to be a project engineer. His management took the suggestion more seriously, and a few months after the article appeared, they offered the author a post as project manager. In another instance, the author, a metallurgist, received no indication that any of his professional colleagues had even seen the article, although that article received top rating in a reader survey conducted by the journal; and later the author's management gave him a slight promotion that expanded his responsibilities to include writing.

With so many possibilities involved in the creation and publication of an article, the statistical odds tilt against the successful prediction of that article's effect. Although the primary payment has been described as prestige, there remains an unresolved roster of qualifications for that prestige. Prestige with whom, for what, and how much of it? Many professional people who have written will advise others that the first article should be considered an exercise in which the experience of writing and publishing is more than half the compensation. However, this book assumes a greater responsibility for its readers, and would advise writers how to achieve a successful publication the first time, as well as how to gain experience by making some generalizations. The key to these generalizations is hindsight; and the reader is asked, at this point, to engage in imaginary hindsight. Put the whole of the creative writing and publishing process into one primitive blob in the mind, imagine there has been no response to a published article, and ask yourself what went wrong.

The fulcrum across which success and failure in publication are balanced resides in that first step of the "Procedure for Prose Composition" in Chapter 2: to establish an audience for the article by both field and function, as well as a subject of interest to that audience and the reason for that interest. At the time, that step seemed difficult. Now, after carrying the chosen subject to a journal which was selected to provide the chosen audience, and after unsuccessful publication in that journal, we find it necessary to add some important questions to that first step.

In order to benefit from that article, the author needs to ask: What is my relation to that audience? Or, more specifically, what are my skills worth to that audience? Or, still more specifically, how will that audience compensate me for those of my skills given prestige through this article? If you master the procedures between that first step of composition and this point of hindsight, you can follow these questions and their answers like a trial-and-error calculation that fixes not only the subject, the composition, and the exposition, but also the journal, the category of article within that journal, and the decisions about handling reprints and tearsheets.

To perform this trial-and-error exercise, you need to step outside yourself, and consider how you may appear to others. Jean Piaget devised an interesting test in this regard. He would ask little children to indicate first their right hand and then their left hand. Then he would place two children face to face and ask them to indicate the facing child's right and left hands. He found that up until the age of about six, children were able only to indicate a mirror image of their own right and left hands, but after about six years of age children could objectively imagine themselves in the place of a facing partner and indicate that partner's right and left hands. The questions about how an author is regarded by an audience of an article require that the author use similar objectivity in analyzing him/her self from the point of view of the projected audience.

To illustrate, the metallurgist mentioned above worked for an engineering company. He was a practiced writer. I discovered a paper he had presented to the National Association of Corrosion Engineers (NACE), and asked him if he would provide an article of fundamentals for the Materials Engineering Forum section of *Chemical Engineering*. He agreed and forthwith provided me with an excellent article—thorough and so well written that I could find no excuse to reorganize it with SPRI. Enthusiastic, I obtained preferential treatment for that article, and after publication, it lived up to expectations. Although corrosion and metallurgy are of secondary interest to chemical engineers, that article appeared at the very top of the readership survey rating, ahead of news and of features more closely oriented to the profession. I was certain that the author would receive many favorable comments and turned to other concerns. However, about six months later, he telephoned me to ask me about reactions to his article. When I described the high readership rating, he was surprised, because he had not received a single comment, and his previous papers had all drawn much comment. He added a bit wryly that, apparently because of the article, he had received a minor promotion that he did not want.

This incident reveals much about: (1) choice of a subject; (2) choice of a publication for an article; and (3) the position of an author relative to the audience by which the article was received. Once we have identified these effects, you should be able to apply them to your own position, your skills and an article you might write.

First of all, the article treated fundamentals of corrosion science; it appeared in a department, called Materials Engineering Forum in a journal called *Chemical Engineering*. This is a route to publication recommended earlier in this chapter. By publishing in a department, the author avoided reviews by anonymous editors; and this article was actually solicited by the department editor, who took pains to see that the article was well presented in the magazine. This resulted in a high readership rating, but beyond that, nothing. Why?

Consider the author's skills in relation to his audience. He was employed as a staff consultant metallurgist in a large engineering company devoted to the design of refineries and petrochemical plants. His article was devoted to fundamentals and perhaps was redundant to other metallurgists. His audience was composed of chemical engineers, who generally performed the same functions as the engineers of the company where he was employed—perhaps even competing with the engineers of his own company. Few of his professional colleagues in metallurgy even saw the article, because they subscribed to publications of the NACE, where he had previously appeared and enjoyed correspondence. Although the audience that did see the article might have felt a desire to avail themselves of further advice or the author's services, they were hardly in a position to do so, or even to write him at his place of employment in a competitive company. With all this hindsight, the wonder is that the author's own company approved publication of the article; they would have done better to reproduce it and distribute it privately to their own chemical engineers, who probably did clip his article from the magazine.

From this point of view, we begin to see a shrewder attitude that can be applied during that first step of prose composition. In addition to establishing an audience, subject, and interest, authors should ask what they meant to and are able to do for the selected audience. For example, self-employed accountants, doctors, and lawyers should look beyond the professional journals of their own fields, and seek out departments in journals serving related fields, where a careful presentation of the fundamentals of an author's profession would be received with intense interest. Also, the first impulse of a physicist who has just obtained a masters degree in business administration might be to write for newly acquired MBA colleagues. However that would be much less effective than writing for physicists to tell them something of what had been learned in acquiring the MBA.

In applying this point of view, it is of course necessary to consider one's place of employment. In Chapter 5, we saw an incident in which four cost engineers had presented for their society a study of the relative effects of variations in investment costs, feedback costs, and price. The mechanisms of the study comprised conventional calculations for return on investment based on discounted cash flow. Those calculations are so familiar that their colleagues may have yawned in the authors' faces; and those colleagues were not interested in the results. However, those results were picked up by a journal devoted to executive-level subscribers, where its reception was most favorable. During subsequent meetings with the four authors, all mentioned a new popularity in their corporations, and one of the four said that, because of the publication, he had had a meeting with the corporation's president, who previously had not even known his name. It was partly this potential for effectiveness that made our failure to produce more articles so frustrating for me; and it was probably a lack of respect for publication outside their profession that made the four engineers less eager to produce.

In addition to a shrewder choice of audience, the successful author needs to make a careful choice of appropriate facts with which to attract that audience in the situation of an article. Although those facts need not affect the language of an article, they do set the tone in a manner that less informed people might ascribe to style. The effect is well demonstrated by comparing two articles, one on the use of energy,[1] and the other on molecular sieve catalysts.[2] These articles appear markedly different, but they have so many points in common that each can be taken as an analogy for the other. Some of their common points are:

1. Both are composed according to the situation-problem-resolution-information structure, by the same author.
2. Both treat complex subjects—one molecular sieve catalysis, the other energy handling equipment—in the information category of the article's structure.

3. Both use a relatively simple resolution—an equilateral pyramid for the molecular sieves, and a heat balance for the energy equipment—through which to engage the reader with the necessarily complex descriptions.
4. Both were featured in the issues of the magazines in which they appeared.
5. Both articles spoke to a large portion of the subscribers of the magazines.
6. Both articles addressed a timely interest, which on the one hand was a new family of catalysts and on the other hand a means for surviving the energy crisis.

With so much in common, one might assume similar successes for the two articles. In fact one was highly successful, but the other was a dud. One of the companies interviewed for the catalyst article had decided at the last minute to forgo a press conference and advertising campaign for announcing its entry into the field of catalysis, and to depend instead on the effects of the article. This was a classic choice between public relations and advertising, and the company conducted a series of surveys to discover if its decision had been correct. Those surveys revealed what would be considered a high readership rating, and showed that a single, well-read article was as effective as an expensive advertising campaign. By contrast, the readership rating of the energy article was mediocre; and considering the timeliness of the subject and that this article was featured in its issue of the magazine, that mediocre rating should be interpreted as a failure.

It was tempting to blame this failure on the complexity of the subject, and that conclusion was arrived at by some. However, the same author had achieved success with an equally complex subject in the article on catalysts. There had to be another explanation, which could only be revealed by a more careful analysis. Such an analysis is possible with SPRI, and it shows a secondary advantage from thinking in terms of thought classes. The key to the success and failure is found in the articles' situations, one of which was busy, and the other pedantic. Both articles had been based on information contributed by a number of companies active in the field; in both articles, that contributed information comprised the information section of the SPRI form. However, in the catalyst article, an unusually long situation was formed of descriptions of concurrent activities of the companies that contributed the information. From those descriptions, it was natural to present the problem as the common element in all the activity.

It would have been equally suitable to describe concurrent activities of the contributors of the energy article, to ask what it was that all these activities had in common, and then to answer that question with the article's resolution, heat balances. However, that article took the approach of describing, as situation, the importance of energy in companies' economics, and then describing, as problem, the need to account for energy consumed and delivered.

There are broader implications from this comparison. Trained professionals generally need to focus attention in applying their skills. Consequently, there is a tendency among the professional writers to express everything in terms of abstractions. However, this tendency runs counter to the whole purpose of publishing, which is for people; and authors for the professional journals should try to express their chosen subjects in terms of people.

In sum, successful publication depends on offering a good article to an appropriate audience. This means that a choice of subject for the article should anticipate a preferred journal, the means of approaching that journal, how the specific audience relates to the author, the subjects handled by the various parts of the journal, and how to compete for the attention of the specific audience. In order to put these parts into closer perspective, we might use some feedback for Chapters 5 and 6.

FEEDBACK FOR CHAPTERS 5 AND 6

The relation between the last two chapters and Chapters 1 through 4 offers an effective demonstration of the "contingent" uncertainty of information theorists.[3] Chapters 1 through 4 dealt with writing, Chapters 4 and 5 with getting published. Each of the two groups of chapters discusses a distinct subject and is internally tied together through related problems and resolutions that correspond to the information theorists' "conditional" uncertainty. However, successful publication depends on, first, a successful choice of subject for composition and, second, the choice of conditions described in the situation category of an SPRI article. These two points are the contingencies through which Chapters 1 through 4 become dependent on Chapters 5 and 6, and vice versa.

Taking an overall view of a complete writing and publishing project, we now see that a trained professional might begin with an idea that spoke to an audience identified by a department of a journal, and then cast about for a suitable combination of situation and problem, both to bring out this idea, as resolution, and to relate that resolution to the chosen audience. We saw in Chapter 2 that the statement of a problem tends to separate the composition into two groups of thought modifiers, the same as the subject and verb of an English sentence separate the sentence into two groups of word modifiers.

In Chapters 5 and 6 we find two contingencies relating three subgroups of conditional information. We found that, first, an author needs to select a journal and, second, the author's manuscript needs to be accepted, after which it becomes necessary to compete for the attention of subscribers. In this case, the contingencies are the desired subscriber-readers, whom the author approaches in the manner of an advertiser, and the specific editors and departments of a journal, which must carry the article to the desired reader-subscribers.

Chapter 5 began with a statement of the overall problem: Why publish? Why not stop with creating an article? An actual incident involving the promulgation of an ammonia manufacturing process was used to demonstrate that the author's payment for publication comes in the prestige afforded by that publication. This notion of payment in prestige was carried through to the final section of Chapter 6, "Hindsight to the Fore," where some actual incidents were used to demonstrate that prestige means nothing to an author, unless it is created among people in the position to make use of something the author is in the position to offer.

The search for a prestigious journal for preferred publication was described in Chapter 5. This took us to "Reading Between the Pages," where two checklists were offered: (1) identify a suitable journal; and (2) qualify the identified journal through its advertisements.

The suggestion that an author might have difficulty finding a suitable journal next led to a discussion of publishing a book. By way of demonstrating the desired composition of a book, this book was compared with two of its primary references. The chores required of an author of a book were described. The high cost of camera-ready illustrations was seen as a deterrent to this type of publication.

Returning to publishing in a professional journal, we next considered editing, an aspect of journal publishing that may seem an unnecessary evil to many authors. Why edit? It was pointed out that, whereas the manuscript for an article may belong to its author, the journal for publishing that article belongs to the editor. Whereas the author chooses a journal for its prestige, the proper responsibility for that prestige belongs to the editor, who accepts many articles to form the journal's contents for issue after issue. Accepting editors and editing as a necessary aspect of publishing, we tried to understand them through an analogy with banking. This led us to see the editors' outstanding characteristics as cautiousness and conservatism.

As a means toward working out the complex considerations of choosing a journal, we considered public relations, and saw that such people introduce another contingency, which can be useful through a broad knowledge of writing, of publishing, and of commercial companies.

This led us to assume, at the beginning of Chapter 6, that we had settled on three or four possible journals, and to ask what we should do next. That led to a fictional account of an ideal publishing experience, which involved an author, the author's boss, the author's company, a staff public relations woman, two editors, their journal, and a series of articles. This fictional ideal revealed the five necessary steps toward getting published: to write, to show authority, to get one's article reviewed, to get the article scheduled, and to get edited. In addition, it revealed important qualifiers such as the author's employment, the relation to publishing of the author's employer, the availability of an interested public relations person, and the immediate personal effects of an interest in writing. We saw that an author's most important abilities are: to write, to discuss, to separate regular work from writing, to invent, to explain, to be self-effacing, to be patient, and to be persistent.

Unfortunately, real life hardly ever matches an ideal. In order to be practical, it became necessary to measure the situation of any author against the necessities of publishing. These practical necessities were listed as ten functions necessary to editing a journal, plus twelve steps that an article must pass through between submission and reader reaction. These plus some practices common in industry identified three routes toward a prestigious publication, as follows:

1. Get the journal to plan an article subject, get appointed as author for that subject, and get the article scheduled. Then write the article.
2. Write an unsolicited article and submit it.
3. Discover in back issues of the journal a suitable subject with which the journal maintains an association, and propose yourself as author for a repeat of that subject.

With an article published through a sympathetic editor, we then assumed that the article had failed to obtain the desired response, and made some analyses of what might have happened, reconsidering the actual publishing activities that had just been reviewed. These analyses showed that: (1) a shrewd author might do better to publish an article for a related field; and (2) the material presented in an article's situation category of thoughts should be chosen to interest the projected audience.

That just about completes instructions for how to write for the professional journals, except for one important factor: Good luck. I wish you lots of it.

NOTES

CHAPTER 1

1. Ryle Miller, Jr., "Process Energy Systems," *Chemical Engineering* (May 20, 1968): 130–48.
2. Samuel Strelzoff, *Technology and Manufacture of Ammonia* (New York: John Wiley & Sons, 1981), 197–198.
3. Robert Graves and Alan Hodge, *The Reader Over Your Shoulder: A Handbook for Writers of English Prose* (New York: Macmillan, 1943), 127.
4. L. S. Vigotsky, *Thought and Language* (New York: MIT Press/John Wiley & Sons, 1962), 33.
5. Wendell R. Garner, *Uncertainty and Structure as Psychological Concepts* (New York: John Wiley & Sons, 1962), 162–166.
6. Heniz Werner, *Comparative Psychology of Mental Development* (New York: International Universities Press, 1948), 55.
7. H. A. Witkin et al. *Psychological Differentiation* (New York: John Wiley & Sons, 1962), 7–23.
8. Kurt Goldstein, *The Organism* (New York: American Book Co., 1939).
9. Garner, *Uncertainty and Structure*, 96.

CHAPTER 2

1. Garner, *Uncertainty and Structure*, 310.
2. Vigotsky, *Thought and Language*, 56–57.
3. Stephen Ullmann, *Style in the French Novel* (London: Cambridge University Press, 1957), 214.
4. James J. Gibson, *The Senses Considered as Perceptual Systems* (Boston: Houghton-Mifflin, 1966), 31.

CHAPTER 3

1. Garner, *Uncertainty and Structure*.
2. Strelzoff, *Technology and Manufacture of Ammonia*.
3. Graves and Hodge, *Reader Over Your Shoulder*.
4. Hadley Cantril, *The Morning Notes of Adelbert Ames, Jr.* (New Brunswick, N.J.: Rutgers University Press, 1960), 4.
5. Charles C. Fries, *The Structure of English* (New York: Harper & Brothers, 1952), 258–259.
6. Ibid., 261.
7. Gibson, *The Senses Considered as Perceptual Systems*, 31–32.
8. Graves and Hodge, *Reader Over Your Shoulder*, 137.
9. Alain Chauvel et al., *Manual of Economic Analysis of Chemical Processes* (New York: McGraw-Hill, 1981), ix.
10. Dudley B. Smith and Ryle Miller, Jr., "The Buying and Selling of Concepts," *Chemical Engineering* (Sept. 25, 1967): 140.
11. Strelzoff, *Technology and Manufacture of Ammonia*, v.
12. Graves and Hodge, *Reader Over Your Shoulder*, 11.
13. Christopher Morley, *Familiar Quotations by John Bartlett* (Boston: Little, Brown, 1941), 784.
14. Cantril, *Morning Notes*, 4.
15. Raymond W. Short and Richard B. Sewall, *Short Stories for Study* (New York: Henry Holt, 1941), 1.
16. Ibid., 183.
17. Lynn White, Jr., "The Historical Roots of Our Ecologic Crisis," *Science* (March 10, 1967): 1203–1208.
18. Howard Topoff, "Ant Wars," *Natural History* (Jan. 1987): 63.
19. F. S. Macneish, *Civil Engineering in the Process Industries* (London: Leonard Hill, 1968), 1.
20. Vigotsky, *Thought and Language*.

CHAPTER 4

1. Paul Ziff, *Semantic Analysis* (Ithaca: Cornell University Press, 1960), 247.

2. Jean Masseron, *l'Economic des Hydrocarbures* (Paris: Éditions Technique, 1975), extracts, and A. Chauvel, G. Lefebure, L. Castex, *Procedés de Petrochimie* (Paris: Éditions Technique, 1985), extracts.

CHAPTER 5

1. Miller, "Process Energy Systems."

CHAPTER 6

1. Miller, "Process Energy Systems."
2. Ryle Miller, "Molecular Sieve Catalysts" *Chemical Week* (Nov. 14, 1964):78–85.
3. Garner, *Uncertainty and Structure*.

EXERCISES: EXAMPLES FOR CHAPTER 3

White Sauce

Some people characterize French cooking as cooking based on sauces thickened with flour. If so, white sauce, with its relative, brown sauce, is the basis for French cooking. White sauce is used in making soups, a wide variety of much used sauces, soufflés, and even puff pastry. The fundamental part of any white sauce consists of a smooth mixture of flour in an appropriate liquid, such as chicken broth, cream, egg yolk and cream, tomato puree, seasoned and cooked white wine, fish stock, and so on, as well as thickeners like cheese to prepare sauces for gratinéeing.

No matter which of these preparations is intended, however, the preparation of white sauce faces one common problem—the raw pasty taste characteristic of flour before it is cooked or baked. In order to achieve delicious flavors, this characteristic flour taste must be removed; and that means the flour must somehow be cooked—enough to eliminate the raw taste without turning the flour brown.

In the past, in the luxurious kitchens of the European aristocracy, the raw taste was cooked out of flour by simmering the near-finished sauce for several hours over a low flame. However, this method, which results in the French *sauce velouté*, has drawbacks. It takes time, thus interfering with the preparation of derivative sauces; and it is relatively awkward, because thick sauces simmer differently than thin sauces. Consequently most contemporary white sauces are made through an equivalent flour-cooking procedure, known by its French name, *roux*. Cooking the *roux* is the critical step in the preparation of a white sauce.

To make a *roux*, flour is gently cooked in butter. Butter is essential because of its sharply defined cooking temperatures; first, it melts; after continued heating, the melted butter begins to froth and bubble; after still further gentle heating, whitish milky substances separate in the froth leaving clarified butter beneath; and after still further heating the clarified butter turns brown. Relative to this scale of butter temperatures, flour loses its taste when heated to the point at which butter froths; further heating, to the point at which clarified butter is formed, causes the flour to turn golden brown; and still further heating causes both the flour and the milky substances separated from the butter to brown to an unpleasant bitter taste.

Accordingly, the key to making a good white sauce consists of heating flour in melted butter gently; it requires about 2 minutes for the mixture to begin to froth. The mixture of flour and butter forms a thick paste, which can be pushed into a smear across the bottom of the pan or rolled into globs. Any hot spots in the pan's bottom would brown the smears and globs of *roux*, so that success with white sauce mandates a heavy pan of tin-lined copper, backed stainless steel, or teflon-lined aluminum. Bare aluminum can impart a taste to the delicate *roux*. Also, a wooden spatula is essential for constantly stirring the *roux* during the few minutes it takes to cook it.

Once the *roux* is formed, the pan should be removed from the heat and the liquid for the sauce beaten in with a wire whisk.

The procedure for preparing a white sauce is as follows:

1. Melt butter in a sauce pan over low heat.
2. Add the flour to the melted butter, all at once, with constant stirring, as the *roux* is allowed to form and heat.
3. When, after a few minutes of heating, the *roux* begins to froth, promptly remove the pan from the heat, continuing to work the *roux* until it is cooled slightly.
4. Add the liquid, all at once, beating it into the *roux* with a wire whisk.

Proportions:

The volume of butter should be two-thirds the measured volume of flour.

Each cup of liquid extender requires flour as follows to achieve the desired thickness:

for thin soup—1 tablespoon
for general purpose sauce—1½ tablespoons
for thick sauce—2 tablespoons
for soufflé base—3 tablespoons

Example:

You want to make 2 cups of a thick cream sauce to go over vegetables or eggs. This will require, for liquid, ½ cup of whipping cream, salt, pepper, and lemon juice, plus 1½ cups of thick white sauce. This thick white sauce will require (1½ × 2) = 3 tablespoons of flour, plus (3 × ⅔) = 2 tablespoons of butter. Melt the 2 tablespoons of butter; add the 3 tablespoons of flour; make the *roux*; add the 1½ cups of liquid, beating; beat in cream and seasonings.

Brown Sauce

Practically everyone who has been around a kitchen has admired the delicious glazes of dried juices that coat the inside of a pan in which meat has been browned. Recovering these glazes and converting them into a sauce is at once thrifty, nutritiously rewarding, and tasteful. In America the recovered sauce is known by the broad, all-encompassing name of "gravy." In France it is known as *sauce brune*, or brown sauce, which may be more specifically called *sauce diable*, *sauce piquant*, *sauce Robert*, *sauce à l'estragon*, *sauce duxelles*, or *sauce chasseur*, depending on whether the complementary seasonings are pepper, pickles and capers, mustard, tarragon, mushrooms, or mushrooms with tomatoes, respectively. Whatever the name, brown sauce is one of the delights of occidental cooking; it is almost always served with meat, fowl, or game.

There are times, however, when the sight and taste of gravy do not measure up to the promise of the roasting pan, when the gravy lacks the rich deep color of the roast, is pasty, pale, and fluffy, and tastes unpleasantly of flour. At such times the cook has neglected a primary rule. *Flour must be cooked.* Cooking the flour is a critical step in the preparation of any of the brown sauces or gravies.

Like its relative, white sauce, brown sauce should get its flour via a *roux*, a mixture of flour and shortening. However, the brown sauce flour is cooked to a higher temperature. This means that higher boiling fats and oils can be used in place of butter; and when butter is used, it should first be heated through the frothy stage (at which the white sauce *roux* is made) to make a clarified butter by skimming off the milky substances, which otherwise burn to a bitter taste. The flour is then added to the clarified butter and cooked until it is golden or nut-brown in color. If a taste other than butter is desirable, either rendered pork fat or cooking oil can replace the butter. Also, the proportions are different; a brown sauce *roux* needs 1½ volumes of fat to each volume of flour. In any event, the *roux* is cooked slowly, at an even temperature, with constant working, so that the flour is cooked evenly throughout. As soon as the desired golden color is reached, the *roux* should be removed from the heat and stirred until slightly cooler. Then already boiling stock or bouillon is whipped into this *roux* with a wire whisk. Because the flour of this lightly browned *roux* does not go into its liquid as easily as the paler flour of the white sauce's *roux*, the browned *roux* and its stock or bouillon should finally be simmered for 2 hours, with fat and scum skimmed off as necessary. Thus the step-by-step procedure for preparing a brown sauce is as follows:

1. Obtain a stock or bouillon, bring it to a boil, and let it simmer to one side.
2. Prepare clarified butter, rendered pork fat, or cooking oil in a suitable sauce pan under gentle heat.
3. Add the flour all at once and begin working the fat and the flour together into the *roux*, which can be smeared and rolled about in the pan with a wooden spatula.
4. Carefully heat the *roux*, working it continuously, so that the flour is cooked slowly and evenly to a golden or nut-brown color. This takes 8–10 minutes.
5. As soon as the *roux* has reached its color, remove from the heat and add the simmering stock or bouillon, beating it into the *roux* with a wire whisk.
6. Simmer the brown sauce, partly covered, for 2 hours, skimming off fat and scum as they appear on the surface. Adjust thickness by adding liquid, until a spoon dipped into the sauce carries an even coating on its back.

Proportions:

Each cup of finished sauce requires 1½ cups of stock or bouillon, 1 tablespoon of flour, and 1½ tablespoons of butter or fat.

Example:

To make 4 cups of giblet gravy: Put together 1–4 cups of giblets, bones, and meat trimmings, plus ½ cup each of chopped carrots and onions in a sauce pan. Brown the meat, stirring from time to time. Remove the browned meat to a side dish. Obtain 6 cups of stock or bouillon, dried or canned, bring to a boil, and let simmer to one side. Add enough fat to sauce pan to make up 6 tablespoons, and bring to temperature. Add 4 tablespoons of flour. Cook the *roux* over low heat until it turns golden.

Add the simmering bouillon, plus the browned meat. Simmer for 2 hours. Strain out the solids.

Hollandaise Sauce

Hollandaise sauce, which is also known as egg-yolk-and-butter sauce, is perhaps the most famous of all sauces, particularly when it is realized that bernaise and white wine sauces are merely hollandaise sauce with its lemon-juice seasoning replaced by tarragon and fish stock seasonings, and that mousseline sauce is hollandaise with whipped cream. It is hard to imagine anything richer.

From a cook's point of view, hollandaise sauce unfortunately wins a substantial portion of its fame because of the difficulty of its preparation. The statement of preparation is simple: Prepare an emulsion of melted butter in egg yolks by whipping them together. But a problem lies in the temperature, about 160°F, at which egg yolks are prepared to emulsify the butter. This temperature is hotter than the maximum touch tolerance of the normal human (125–130°F), but is considerably below the boiling point of water (about 210°F). Yet if egg yolks are heated too close to the boiling point of water, they cook; and if they are only warmed past the touch-tolerant temperature, they will not emulsify the butter. Between those two limits, however, the yolks' long protein molecules can be made to go through visible changes that stop short of cooking but do make the yolk a useful emulsifier. Because eggs and egg yolks are so important to good cooking, the familiarity with eggs that is gained by making hollandaise sauce comes as a bonus.

The trick is to know by their appearance when egg yolks go through their transition. First, beat the yolks and watch them become thick and sticky (about 1 minute). Then dilute them slightly with cold water, salt, and lemon juice, and beat them into the slightly thinner mixture. Then add cold butter, and setting the sauce pan or bowl with the yolks in a pan of simmering water, stir the mixture, watching carefully as it thickens to a creamy consistency (1–2 minutes). If the eggs thicken too fast or start to get lumpy, move the sauce pan to a pan of cold water. When the cream is thick enough to let the pan bottom show as the whisk is dragged across it, the yolks are ready to accept the melted butter. Begin by adding some cold water and stirring this in to cool the yolks below their cooking temperature; then add melted butter drop by drop, as it emulsifies, while continuously beating with the wire whisk. Leave out any milky residue that has settled out of the melted butter. If the sauce gets too thick, it can be thinned with hot water, stock, or milk. If the sauce refuses to thicken, warm a mixing bowl by rinsing it with hot water, add a tablespoon of the unthickened sauce with a teaspoon of lemon juice, and beat until it thickens. Then beat in the remainder of unthickened sauce by spoonfuls, as they are emulsified.

The step-by-step procedure for making hollandaise sauce is as follows:

1. Select a stainless steel sauce pan or bowl that will fit into both a pan of simmering water and a bowl of cold water kept handy to the side.
2. Melt the butter and keep it handy to the side.
3. Get ready 2 measures of cold butter.
4. Separate eggs and put the yolks into the pan.
5. Beat the egg yolks cold, for about 1 minute, until they have slightly thickened.
6. Add salt, lemon juice, and water to the beaten egg yolks. Beat for about half a minute more.
7. Add a measure of cold butter and, placing the selected pan or bowl in the simmering water, stir while the butter melts and goes into the yolks. When the mixture becomes creamy and the bottom of the pan or bowl shows behind the whisk, remove from the heat.
8. Add another measure of cold butter and beat it in.
9. Add the melted butter by drops, at the rate that it is taken into the emulsion, while beating continuously with the wire whisk.

Proportions:

A yolk from a large egg will emulsify a maximum of about 6 tablespoons of butter, but 4 tablespoons per yolk are recommended for safety. Lemon juice and cold water are each added at about ½ teaspoon per tablespoon of butter. One cup of hollandaise thus requires about 12 tablespoons of butter, 3 egg yolks, 1 tablespoon of lemon juice, 1 tablespoon of cold water, and salt to taste.

Mayonnaise

Mayonnaise is perhaps the most common of condiment sauces. It is presented in half-gallon jars on supermarket shelves, in crystal serving dishes for accompanying broiled fish, or as a dip in bowls accompanying fresh vegetables. Unfortunately, the concoctions passing as mayonnaise, as well as the recipes for making it, are as varied as the presentations. The different concoctions often lead one to think that mayonnaise is less than the delight that it is; and the different recipes lend the notion of making mayonnaise an aura of mystery, whereas mayonnaise is in fact almost simpler than boiling an egg.

What has confused so many people about mayonnaise is that it is an emulsion. Given experience in thickening sauces with flour or starch, many people approach mayonnaise in the same fashion. They seek to thicken oil, or oil and water, with an egg, or with egg and flour, even cooking the mixture as they might a white sauce. However, the problem of preparing mayonnaise should be approached from the opposite direction, from the point of view of a salad dressing. When oil and vinegar are combined, as for a dressing, one usually obtains a cloudy or milky emulsion of tiny oil droplets spread through the vinegar; and this emulsion may hold for several minutes. If vinegar is combined with some ingredient that has long molecules that cling to the microscopic oil droplets, one might be able to form an emulsion that is more stable.

In European kitchens in the past, vinegar was supplemented with egg yolks; trial and error through the years showed that 1 large yolk and 1 tablespoon of vinegar will emulsify ¾ cup of oil; and if the yolk and vinegar are beaten together first to prepare the yolk's protein molecules, it is not even necessary to heat the oil. Usually, if the oil is added in a thin stream, it will go into emulsion simply by stirring with a wooden spatula. Furthermore, any of a wide variety of herbs and seasonings seem to help the emulsifying powers of the yolk-vinegar mixture, so that one can easily make a mayonnaise seasoned with salt, pepper, mustard, lemon juice, parsley, oregano, tarragon, chopped shallots, chopped green onions, capers, and so forth.

It is necessary to bear in mind that mayonnaise, like any emulsion, tends to separate on being chilled. So it is easy to put a mayonnaise away in the refrigerator for a day or so, and then, after taking it out, to thoughtlessly give it a whip with a fork and convert it to a cup of cold oil with yellow stuff floating in it. But the separated mayonnaise can be recovered as easily as it is made. Warm a bowl with hot water and dry it; put a spoon of mustard or hot vinegar in the bowl, and gradually beat in the turned mayonnaise with a wire whisk.

The detailed step-by-step procedure for making mayonnaise is as follows:

1. Obtain a warm, dry mixing bowl.
2. Separate an egg and put the yolk in the bowl.
3. Add vinegar, salt, and pepper, and other desired seasonings to taste.
4. Whip the yolk-vinegar mixture until the yolk seems sticky and stringy.
5. Measure ¾ cup of oil or slightly less.
6. Stirring continuously, add the oil to the yolk-vinegar mixture in a fine stream, but never faster than the oil can go into emulsion.
7. Stop blending at intervals to taste, so as not to make the mayonnaise too oily.

Proportions:

Mayonnaise, cups	Vinegar, tablespoons	Oil, cups	U.S. Large egg yolks
1¾	2–3	1½	2
2¾	3–5	2¼	3
3⅔	4–6	3	4

Light Custard Sauce

During late summer and early fall, when peaches, strawberries, blueberries, and other fruits and berries are in season, this sweet cream sauce is practically ubiquitous. It has a slight, sweet, creamy taste that can enhance most any delicate berry without interfering with that berry's natural taste.

Unfortunately, this custard is not easy to prepare; and the frequent shortcuts and safety measures (usually based on flour) used in making it often lead to custard sauces that are not nearly so good as the genuine item. The problem lies in getting the custard to the right thickness.

As with mousseline sauce, the key step in preparing a custard sauce consists of heating egg yolks to the temperature (160°F) at which they will thicken but not scramble. However, this key step is more difficult with custard sauce than with mousseline. Whereas the egg yolks heated for a mousseline carry only lemon juice and salt, those of a custard sauce carry over six times their volume in dissolved sugar and milk. All this volume interferes with a clear perception of the moment when the yolks turn creamy; and it also slows down the rate of heating over simmering water.

Because of such problems, mastering the preparation of a custard sauce establishes a cook's skill with egg yolks; and a genuine custard sauce is an accomplishment to be proud of as well as a delight to eat. The preparation begins with bringing milk to a boil and putting the hot milk handy to one side. The eggs are separated, and the yolks whipped until sticky with a wire whisk. Granulated sugar is added gradually to the whipped yolks, and this mixture beaten until a creamy stream of yolk and sugar running off the whip is thick enough to leave a ribbon sitting on top of the mixture in the bowl. Next, the hot milk is added to the mixture in a thin stream that is continuously whipped in. This causes the mixture to become slightly fluffy but thinner.

Next comes the critical step—heating the custard. This is done either in a thin-walled stainless steel bowl over simmering water, or in a thick-walled sauce pan over direct heat. A candy thermometer may be used, but it is difficult to determine the average overall temperature of the custard with a thermometer. The best method of heating and measuring the temperature depends on the temperament of the cook. As the custard is heated, no areas of the bowl or pan should be left unscraped by the wooden spatula. This ensures that the heat is even throughout the custard. Once the sauce has reached the desired thickness, evenly coating the spatula, it should be removed from the heat and beaten 1–2 minutes to cool it. Just to be sure that it holds no cooked yolks, it can be strained through a sieve. At this point it is ready to receive flavorings, such as chocolate, kirsch, cognac, rum, instant coffee, and so forth.

The step-by-step procedure is as follows:

1. Boil milk and set it aside.
2. Select a thick-walled sauce pan or a thin-walled bowl, depending on the method of heating.
3. Separate eggs; put yolks in the pan/bowl; whip them.
4. Gradually beat sugar into the yolks and continue beating until a ribbon is formed.
5. Gradually add hot milk, while beating, to complete the custard mix.
6. Put custard mix over the heat and continuously scrape sides and bottom of the pan/bowl, while stirring.
7. When the custard is creamy, remove from heat; beat 1–2 minutes to cook; add seasonings.

Proportions:

For 2 cups of custard: 1¾ cup of milk; ½ cup of granulated sugar; 4 egg yolks; and if desired, one of 3 squares of semisweet chocolate, 1 teaspoon of vanilla, 2 tablespoons of kirsch, cognac, or rum.

EXERCISES: EXAMPLES FOR CHAPTER 4

A Brief History of the Petroleum Industry

Petroleum refining is a heavy industry and subject to the same constraints as other heavy industries. However, the refining operation adds a relatively small increase in value to the material processed; crude oil worth $100 is converted into products whose average value is $110, before adding taxes and distribution costs. This low margin of cost benefit causes refiners to lack flexibility. Therefore, petroleum companies are large, integrated, and international. The annual list of largest companies published by *Fortune* magazine includes four oil companies among the top ten, and twelve oil companies among the top fifty. In 1973, the eight largest oil companies accounted for 70 percent of the non-communist world's crude oil production, 60 percent of the refining, and more than 60 percent of the marketed products.

Comment. The original text leaves dangling several propositions that should either be made less remarkable or be accompanied by more information. "A heavy industry whose characteristics are conventional" creates uncertainty about the characteristics of heavy industries in general. What are they? Since a statement of those characteristics would digress from the thrust of the text, the edited version eliminates the word *characteristics*, in favor of *a conventional heavy industry*. The increment by which manufacturers increase the values of raw materials is a criterion often used to characterize the manufacturers, because this increment has implications about other aspects of the operation. Thus petroleum refining consists principally of separating crude oil into more useful components without changing it. The edited version skims over another unresolved uncertainty, with "Therefore petroleum companies are large." Why *therefore*? Is it simply that a large operation is needed to make an equivalent amount of money? A more careful transposition would either eliminate or resolve this uncertainty.

The petroleum industry was born in the United States at a time when there were little or no restrictions to the size and scope of the great trust companies. The Standard Oil Company created by John Davidson Rockefeller (1839–1937) was typical of such trusts. In building his trust, Rockefeller sought to eliminate the restraints to growth. Recognizing that crude oil needed to be refined into products before it could be sold, he saw it was necessary to monopolize refining and to keep to a minimum the costs of transporting the crude from its source to the refinery. Accordingly, the Standard Oil Company of Ohio (founded 1870) used lower transportation costs to sell at lower prices than the small refiners and then absorb those refiners. Ever since 1875, Rockefeller has controlled one-fifth of the American refineries, and in 1979 his company benefited further from the development of pipeline transportation, which further reduced the transportation costs for large refineries.

Comment. This passage is interesting in that it reveals a fundamental difference between typical French and typical American texts. The French texts treat aspects of a situation as parts of a logical construction, whereas Americans tend to treat the same aspects of the same situation as related phenomena. Although these two points of view make little difference to practical activities, they do make a difference in the way the same idea is expressed in a text. Thus the edited version changes "it was possible" to "little or no restrictions," and "bottlenecks of this budding industry" is changed to "the restraints to growth." Also, "bottlenecks to the budding industry" represents a confusing compounded metaphor. Neither a budding plant nor growth experience bottlenecks. Budding occurs as a plant reaches maturity. And the growth of a plant is not a good analogy for the growth of a trust.

John D. Rockefeller thus based his domination of the petroleum industry on controlling crude oil transportation and refining, and on the total absorption of the competitors. By contrast, Henri Deterding, founder of Royal Dutch Shell, followed a very different route toward the same end, in order to establish Royal Dutch Shell as an international enterprise. Whereas Rockefeller operated essentially on the U.S. market, Deterding very quickly brought the international markets under his domination according to what might be termed a one-to-one principle; he arranged to supply specific markets from the nearest source of crude oil. This meant a large number of crude oil production fields well distributed around the entire world according to the probable market. Deterding's principle of operation was suited to the isolated crude oil production fields in the underdeveloped countries, as they existed at the beginning of the twentieth century. These fields in the Dutch East Indies, Mexico, Venezuela, Persia, and so on, were easy to control, because of the high overall transportation costs at that time; and the corresponding markets came naturally under the domination of the companies of the Shell group, which associated with local companies rather than absorbing them.

Comment. This paragraph demonstrates a source of the popular attitude toward metaphor as a key feature of style. Because the two sides of a metaphor share as a common basis, a tenor (a feature selected for comparison), and a vehicle (the projection), it is possible to choose metaphors so that real events are subtly bent at each of these points to suit an author's inclination. Thus at the beginning of this paragraph we again have the French author using a logic that is not perceived by Americans. "The method used by J. D. Rockefeller for dominating" is a metaphor of the actual events. It implies the common ground between a sequence of events and that sequence seen as a pattern of events. This is done through the use of *method used*. This *method used* becomes the tenor, through which we arrive at the projected domination as something calculated. However, this metaphor pretends that Rockefeller knew by foresight what the world knows by hindsight; by attributing the *method used* to Rockefeller, the metaphor pretends he had everything worked out in advance. A French reader might believe that, but an American might reject that notion in favor of the notion that Rockefeller reacted shrewdly to phenomena as they presented themselves. The transposed text allows American readers to make this interpretation.

A similar metaphor is introduced for Henri Deterding as "followed a method" rather than "carry out a policy." (Note that metaphors such as these do survive translation.) This metaphor not only attributes to Deterding the same omniscience accorded Rockefeller, it also gets awkward when it is compounded with another metaphor, "to arrive," so the transposition simplifies this to "followed a route toward." Again, when the French text says Deterding very quickly understood, we have a suggestion of omniscience that is not easily accepted by Americans, so the transposition substitutes action for thought with "brought the international market under his domination."

One might object that this transposition usurps the author's right to his own style, even if that style is in error. If this were a work of fiction, that objection would certainly be viable. However the purpose of a technical text is to transmit information, not to expose an author's style. Also, we have seen under "Meaning Is Where You Find It" in Chapter 4 that there is an individual style to thinking. Other instances where the example transposition converts a logical construct to related phenomena will be apparent.

The changes in word order represent effects of French versus English grammar. Because of accords made through gender and verb tense, the French organization used in the literal translations leads to ambiguity for Americans. Thus "zones of production" become "production zones" and so forth.

Another important difference between J. D. Rockefeller and H. Deterding is seen in their relationship with their governments. For J. D. Rockefeller the government was an obstacle in terms of fiscal constraints and legal constraints stemming from the Sherman Act. For H. Deterding the government was a diplomatic, moral, and even financial support. Within these roles of governments lies the germ of the current problems in the relations between the oil companies and the governments of the large consumer countries. With the birth of British Petroleum in the fall of 1913, international oil lost its character of exclusively private ownership. By 1920, the influence of the United States government was felt by even the American companies, which were strongly regulated by 1943 through the Committee of Foreign Affairs in the Senate. After 1918, the division of Standard Oil under the Sherman Act led to formation of other companies—Texaco, Gulf, Cities Service, Sun Oil, Phillips Petroleum—in the United States, and these rapidly became large international companies because of the expansion of the worldwide markets. The principal product of this market shifted from lamp oil (kerosene) to gasoline, and this shift helped the new companies, because changing markets always help a new company that is less tied to existing investments and therefore more flexible. For example, lamp oil represented 44 percent and gasoline 15 percent of Esso's sales in 1912, while by 1927 gasoline went to 47 percent and lamp oil to 11 percent of those sales.

Comment. Note that, in the sentence beginning "For H. Deterding," the word *it* was changed to *the government*. This change represents perhaps the most common problem of clear writing: making sure that the referents for the *its*, *that, them, they* and so on, are clear. A common exercise in self-editing consists of reviewing each sentence for every one of those function words to see that some other noun has not come between the function word and its referent. If such a noun has come in, either the original noun must be repeated, or (in

English) an accord must be made through singulars and plurals. This principle was mentioned only briefly under "A Hierarchy of Signals," in Chapter 4, so you might need to give it more careful attention here.

An analogous problem appears again in the following sentence of the translation. What is meant by "relationships between companies and the governments of the large consumer countries"? Are those relationships between companies and companies, as well as between companies and governments? Or are they between governments and governments? The transposition tried to resolve this by adding *oil* to describe the companies. Another, perhaps better, way would be to rely on the unique concordance of singulars and plurals in English, and to change *companies* to *a company*; the singular would be understood for *a typical company*, so that the relationship would be understood as between the typical oil company and the governments. In this case, the sentence would read: "Within these roles of a government lies the germ of the current problems to the relationships between a company and the governments of the large consumer countries."

A previous untranslated paragraph mentions that British Petroleum was founded. This was assumed to have taken place in the fall of 1913.

The notion that changing markets aid newcoming companies does not seem to be an economic "phenomenon" to this editor; and the word was replaced with a statement of cause and effect.

The worldwide oil market has been dominated by the contemporary principal international oil companies since the 1930s. These companies were an essential part of the international oil industry, in which integration, concentration, and cooperation are endemic traits. This concentration and cooperation, which could be termed *pact* or *cartel*, results from a need for economic organization. One could say that unrestrained competition is favorable to manufacturing and marketing, but that it is harmful to the exploitation of natural resources. In fact, competition encourages waste at the expense of future generations; it produces instability in raw material markets; and it prevents the necessary heavy investments with their long-term guarantees that are needed for spontaneous fluctuations within the market.

Comment. This paragraph may be strange to Americans, because of the syntax and the sentiments. The first sentence needs complicated transpositions, in order to let the reader instantly know who, what, and when. Then the beginning of the second sentence gives us one of those ambiguous function words. As we have seen in Chapter 4, *they* in that position signals a subsequent sentence. The transposition replaces *they* with *these companies*, so that we know instantly what we are talking about.

After the Second World War, the principal product of the hydrocarbon market changed once again, this time from gasoline to fuels. In addition, some of the consuming countries encouraged the development of new national oil companies, for the purpose of economic security. Similarly, producing countries who sought to better control a key industry for their future development also formed new national oil companies. Because of the existing companies' large investment in conventional production, the new shift in principal product aided the new national oil companies.

Comment. Again, the use of *center of gravity* to mean the principal product is an ambiguous metaphor. In the same sentence, the passive verb *displaced* suggests that the market demand can be willfully manipulated, so that word was changed to *changed* in the active form. Another substitution for the same word is *shifted*, later on. In the next sentence, the function word, *for*, signals a word group that modifies the verb *encouraged*; this word group was transposed to a position on the verb's side of the subject-verb bridge. In the next sentence, neither the use of *It is the same*, nor of *similarly* can avoid ambiguity, and it was necessary to add the phrase, "also formed new national oil companies." In the next sentence the word *size* was interpreted to mean *large investment*, which caused the large companies to be less flexible.

What, then, can be described as the principal characteristics of an international oil company? Without doubt, the first characteristic is integration from exploration through marketing. Integration not only distributes the high risks of crude oil exploration and production over a wider roster of activities, but it also creates one integral industrial chain from exploration to consumers, which protects a company from outside economic interference that would be felt throughout the whole of the company's activities. The second characteristic consists of the diversity and extent of a company's crude oil resources. The supply of crude should be worldwide, like that developed by Deterding, and it should include large zones such as the Near East, Venezuela, and Africa.

The third is the diversity and extent of the market for the finished products. A worldwide market base is not enough. It is also necessary to have a wide range of products, including petrochemicals as well as gasoline and fuel.

The fourth is the minimum economic size, not only internationally but especially in each geographic zone of operation, as well as within each one and for each phase of production.

The final characteristic consists of an international trade name and international symbol creating consumer confidence. Creating that name and symbol is a very important task whose complexity often escapes the non-specialist. The psychological significance of the color of a trademark, for example, must be favorable for all areas of the world, in spite of local mentalities and reactions that are often different. The cost of publicity and change in service stations is always very high. For example, in order to transform the network of Esso, Humble, and Enco into Exxon, up to $100 million was needed for the United States alone.

Comment. After presenting integration as the first characteristic, the original text substitutes the metaphor, *industrial chain* for the word *integration*. This metaphor becomes ambiguous, because it is presented as its negative, a chain with a missing link. It has been necessary both to establish the relation between the sides of the metaphor (integration vs. chain) and to make the action of the chain positive. Near the end of the sentence, the word *its* is used to refer back to *company*. This usage is syntactically correct, *its* and *company* being separated by no other singular nouns; however this separation is so long as to tax a reader's memory, so *its* has been replaced by *the company's*.

Whenever a series of descriptions is used for distinct features of a given item, the reader should be reminded what the descriptions refer to. For this transposition, it was felt that the word *characteristic* needed repeating in the first, second, and final descriptions. The second description uses *its* when it was felt that *a company's* was needed. Also in the second description, the suggestion of a master plan was changed to the suggestion of a consistent policy by changing *the idea* of Deterding to *developed by* Deterding. The second and third descriptions repeat *diversity* and *extent*; and some writers might eliminate those words as redundant. In the final paragraph, the original text grows ambiguous with the expression *therein lies*, so that has been replaced by "Creating that name and symbol is...."

In the 1960s, the choice of petrochemical raw materials lay between two distinct possibilities: ethane and naphtha. The United States had built its petrochemical industry on ethane, because the large U.S. natural gas fields, which supplied gas fuel through a pipeline network, by-produced ethane under good economics through separation at the gas fields. This ethane by-product was well adapted to the manufacture of ethylene.

Europe and Japan, by contrast, did not have large natural gas fields; but they did have supplies of naphtha by-produced from refining crude oil for heavy fuels. The supply of this naphtha exceeded that needed for the motor fuels market, so that it became the principal feedstock for ethylene production in Europe and Japan. Cracking naphtha to ethylene coproduces propylene, butadiene, and benzene; and the price of naphtha was close to that of a fuel ($18/ton in April 1971). This combination of low feedstock price plus the valuable derivatives of naphtha cracking led to a spectacular development of the European and Japanese petrochemical industry, not only of the derivatives of ethylene but also those of propylene, butadiene, and benzene. This development led in turn to a rapid increase in the consumption of petrochemical products for making rubber and plastics, such that the price of naphtha rose from $42/ton in April 1972, on the Rotterdam market to $65/ton by July 1973. The petroleum supply crisis at the end of 1973 amplified this trend, so that the price of naphtha rose rapidly to $130/ton at the end of 1974, and today is about $240/ton.

Comment. These paragraphs have been generally reorganized to change the style from scholarly to technical. The direct translation treats events passively and from a distance through use of such terms as *concerning, there were two directions to take, necessary for satisfying*, and so forth. These terms, which are redundant, have been removed, so that the revolving situations could be described in terms of the action as it occurred. This same transposition from scholarly observation to technical participation required that the events be presented in order of the cause and effect of feedstock and product.

This increase in naphtha price led the petrochemical producer to look for alternate feedstocks that were cheaper but also able to co-produce the derivatives needed by the market. Thus, since 1971, producers increasingly used heavier petroleum refining fractions, such as atmospheric gas oil and even heavy gas oil. Following recently improved recovery both of gases associated with the crude oil of the Near East and of the condensed gases associated with the methane of the gas fields of the North Sea and Indonesia, the European and Japanese petrochemical producers have turned to using propane-butane, often mixed with naphtha, and even ethane in the countries bordering the North Sea. However, because the availability and cost of these raw materials could be uncertain and susceptible to variations, there have appeared flexible steam crackers capable of treating in the same unit whatever different raw materials that were chosen by the operator, depending on both the raw material costs and the prices offered for the derivatives from the downstream units. Finally, the oil- and gas-producing countries of the Near East in particular have integrated themselves more and more toward the derivative markets by manufacturing a greater variety of products in new plants producing ethylene by cracking ethane, along with the manufacture of methanol from associated gases. Since the capacities of these new plants far surpass local demands, their products, which are based on cheap local raw materials, compete with the products of the industrial countries.

Comment. The changes made in this paragraph primarily convert the direct translation to a more idiomatic English typical of the American industry. Although you may not be interested in some of the terms of the hydrocarbon industries, you may benefit from noting the extent to which so-called idiomatic language is based on synonyms. Some of those synonyms are as follows:

Situation for *increase in price*
industry for *producer*
look for and *led to* for *changed to*
other raw materials for *alternate feedstocks*
better adapted economically for *cheaper but also able to coproduce*
in the oil fields for *with the crude oil*
oriented itself for *turned*
one saw for *there have appeared*
needs for *the prices offered for*
the downstream for *derivative markets*
more complicated for *a greater variety of*
installations for *plants*
profiting from for *based on*
manufacture for *products*

Although many of these word changes result from a direct translation, you may find a remarkable number of similar word changes possible in your own first drafts of writing. Some texts on English usage grow vehement about the choices between such words, but you would be better off to ignore those texts, to remember that the word you use represents a choice, and to be satisfied that the choice is your choice.

Also, this paragraph has an interesting transposition. Take the original:

> flexible steam crackers capable of treating different raw materials in the same unit that the operator chose,

Because English does not have the French accords between gender and tenses, this phrase is misleading. Experience with steam cracking lets this editor recognize that *the operator chose* must refer to *raw materials*, and not to *the same unit*. Furthermore, *in the same unit* must refer to *capable of treating*. Then, the word *different* is one of those ambiguous words, like *good* and *difficult*, which were discussed under "Meaning Is Where You Find It" in chapter 4, and this phrase offers a practical demonstration of how those words can cause trouble. What is meant by *different*? Are the different raw materials a new class chosen by the operator, or do they vary? We get our clue from the word *flexible*, and accordingly write the phrase as: "flexible steam crackers capable of treating in the same unit whatever different raw materials that were chosen by the operator."

World markets were profoundly disturbed during 1971–1984 by the economic recession and the continual rise in costs of production, which resulted from the rise in price of petroleum raw materials. This rise in costs affected the large markets for intermediate products, particularly in underdeveloped countries. During the 1960s, it was felt that the low cost of petrochemical derivatives, such as fertilizers and polymers, would play a decisive role in the industrial growth of the underdeveloped countries by the end of the century. But projections made at that time are far from being realized. This failure is due to, first, the effects of raw-material costs, which represent 85 percent of the operating cost of a contemporary steam cracker, compared to only 48 percent in 1973. Then, over the same period investments have grown fourfold in discounted currency and by 1.6 fold in constant currency. Because of this, the petrochemical derivatives have lost their suitability for wide distribution in the underdeveloped countries. In the industrial countries, the economic crisis had the consequence of slowing down consumption, so that production capacities remain very much in excess of the demand, which weighs heavily on the financial stability of companies.

Comment. The most interesting part of this paragraph is the lapse of cause and effect at the crux of an important observation. After saying that the hopes of the underdeveloped countries "are far from being accomplished," the original begins a new sentence with, "First of all, the reason can be attributed...." It so happens that this bit of text identifies a major contributor to the African famines so much discussed by the newspapers as this text is being prepared. Thus the lack of accomplishment can accurately be described as a failure.

INDEX

Accidence, 5
Advance against royalties, 116
Advertisers, perceptions of, 110–11
Advertising: content of, 110–11; journal analysis by, 109–12; type of, 110–11; versus public relations, 147; volume of, 109–11
Affiliation, journal, 105
Alice in Wonderland, 87
Ambiguity: for interesting writing, 60–64; lexical, 87–88; that helps, 61; that hinders, 61
Ambiguous words, 173
American Petroleum Institute, 131
Ames, Adelbert, Jr., 60, 78
Analogy between invention and SPRI composition, 92–93
Article outline, 7–8
Articles: *Chemical Week*, 7–8; competition among, 139–43; of concept development, 103; effects of, 7, 101; image–making, 139; per issue, 106; prestige from, 101–4; special treatment of, 141, 142; time required for, 8; unsolicited, 132–33
Articulation, non-verbal, 3
Audience-subject-interest, establishing, 40–41
Authors, book, 114–15

Backlog for publication, 139–41
Beck, Simone, 68
Bertholle, Louisette, 68
Biography, author's, 106
Book publishing, 112–16

Chemical Engineering, 6, 8, 9
Chemical Week, example from, 24
Child, Julia, 68
Choice as characteristic of design, 38–39
Circulation, of journals, 105–6

Index

Clear writing, most common problem of, 168
Concepts: characteristics of, 26–27; circuit of, for writing, 4, 15; destruction of, 23–24; development of, 10–12, 14, 25–26, 28–29; finding questions in, 52–55; as ganglions, 27; metamorphosis through, 28–29; pattern of in NH_3 manufacture, 103; promulgation of, 14, 102–3; scientific, 6; triumvirate for writing, 12; use of, 92
Concordances, 92, 168, 173
Contingency and public relations, 120–21
Copy editing, 72–73

Decentralization, 11
Departments of journals, 133–35
Description: purposeless, 49, 50–51; with abstract purpose, 49, 51; with individual purpose, 49–50, 51–52
Design: assumptions for, 20–21; basis for, 20; calculations for, 19; problem, 21; procedures for, 19–21; refinery, 18–19; results, 21; six criteria for, 20; specific conditions for, 21; prose, 36
Directory of Publishing Opportunities in Journals and Periodicals, 108

Editing, 82; and editors, 117–19; objections to, 10; self, 90; SPRI Method, 9–10
Editor, copy, 115–16; production, 115–16
Editorial functions, 130–33
Egocentric speech, 46, 78, 89, 90
English: orderliness in, 75–81; peculiarities of, 54–55; redundancy in, 61
Ephron, Nora, 40
Ethylene, manufacture of, 23–25
Examples: for exercises for Chapter 3, 155–63; for exercises for Chapter 4, 165–74

Exercises: for Chapter 3, 67–70; for Chapter 4, 94–99

Facts, packaging of, 62–64
Feedback: description of in perception, 37; for Chapter 2, 36–39; for Chapter 3, 64–67; for Chapter 4, 92–94; for Chapters 5 and 6, 148–50
Fluid films, as a concept, 22–23
Form, in language and mathematics, 82
Four, classes of words, 83; rule of, 9
Fries, C. C., 74, 75
Fries' method of analysis, 82–83
Fries' 154 function words, 77–79
Function words, 75–76, 83–86; ambiguous, 169

Galley proofs, 115–16
Goldstein, Kurt, 10
Good, meaning of, 88–89
Gordon, Henry, 72, 73, 74
Grammar, conventional, 81–82
Graves, Robert, 74
Group A function words, 83–84, 85
Group B function words, 84
Group C function words, 84
Group D function words, 84
Group E function words, 84
Group F function words, 75–76, 84–85
Group G function words, 85
Group H function words, 86
Group I function words, 86
Group J function words, 77–79, 86
Group K function words, 86
Group L function words, 86
Group M function words, 86
Group N function words, 86
Group O function words, 86
Guide to Scientific Periodicals, 108

Habits as tools, 15–16
Hardy, Thomas, 61
Hemingway, Ernest, 62
Hemingway's iceburg, 29
Hodge, Alan, 74

Illustration-as-resolution, 32–33
Illustrations, camera-ready, 115–16
Image subjects, 138–39
Immediate constituents, 64
Included sentences as modifiers, 77–78
Index, preparation of, 116
Information: bits of, 14; content, high, 78; as equal opposite of uncertainty, 14; in SPRI, 31–33; theory, 14
Innovations, technical, promulgation of, 104
Issues per year, 105

Jabberwocky, The, 87
Journals: checklist for analysis of, 105; evaluation of, 104–12

M. W. Kellogg Company, 29, 102
Kipling, Rudyard: 55; six serving men, 55; his Ws, 55–60
Know-how, 20; through writing, 35–36

Language, idiomatic, 173
Le Chatelier: and logic, 5, 27; principle of, 5
Letter: of inquiry, 135–36; to accompany manuscript, 137–38
Lexicography, 87
Libraries, 107–8
Linguistic approach to analysis of English, 82
Logic, 5, 6

Mail handling, in journals, 135–36
Masthead titles, glossary of, 118–19
Meaning, 86–91; examples of shift in, 11; partitioning of, 46–47
Memory strain, 171
Metaphor, ambiguous, 170; description of, 27

National Association of Corrosion Engineers, 144, 145
News, 8
Newspapers, five Ws of, 56–58; lead paragraphs in, 56–58; triangular style of, 56–58; writing for, 56

Oblad, Alex, 29–30, 31
O'Hare, Tom E., 103, 104
Order, subject-verb, 92
Orderliness behavior, 13
Orthology, 5

Pedagogy, weakness of, 113
Perception, studies of, 47–48
Petroleum industry, a brief history of, 165–74
Piaget, Jean, 11
Prestige from publishing, 101–4
Primitive mode of thought, 91–92
Problem-resolution: role of, 31–33, 36; stating, 41–42
Problem, pertinent, 107
Problem, research, statement of, 108
Problems, applied, 29–33; metamorphosized, 27
Procedure for composition, example of, 42–44
Professional journals, 117–18; smaller, 122–23
Prognosis in perception, 48
Proprietary technology, disclosure of, 128
Prose, thought-dominated versus language-dominated, 40
Prose composition, 17; criteria for, 39; directing attention in, 52–54; procedure for, 39–44; three-step method for, 54
Proust, Marcel, 58, 90; his use of uncertainty, 58–60
Publication, delays in, 116; successful, 143–48
Public relations, 119–22; fields of, 121–22; staff, 129–39
Publishing: best approach to, 136–37; ideal situation for, 127–29; independent, 133–39; qualifications for, 129–30; requirements for, 129; sequence of events in, 140–43
Purpose: in perception, 48; or prognosis, 88; use in writing

Reader Over Your Shoulder, The, 112–14
Readership surveys, 7, 9, 74
Reporters, types of, 124
Research, library, 106–8
Research, organization for, 29–30
Royalties, book, 116
Rule of four, 9

Scientific and Engineering Literature, 108
Shannon, C. E., 14
Signal and sign, 91
Signals: hierarchy of, 91–92, 168–69; for included sentences, 77–79; for modifying word groups, 75–76; in syntax, 71–74
Signal-words, 74; with no meaning, 81–86
Signification, from problems, 31–33
Situation and information, facts for, 42
Situation in SPRI, 31–33
SPRI (situation, problem, resolution, information): as an aid to clear thinking, 44; editing by, 9–10; effects of, 10; in design thinking, 18–22; in editing, example of, 33–35; objections to, 10; and plagiarizing conference papers, 35
SPRI composition, its strain on syntax, 72–74
Structural meaning, 83
Structure of English, The, 112–13
Style, personal, 79, 89, 91

Subject-verb, order of, 170
Subscriber titles, 41
Syntax, 5
Syntax signals, to mode of thought, 12

Thinking, better-than-average, 114; conceptual, 6; discipline for, 3–5; French, 94–95; in design, 15–22; non-verbal, 3; professional, 3; progress in, 6; tools for, 1, 4
Thought: classes of, 6–10; non-verbal, 46–47; primitive, use of, 73–74; primitive versus cognitive, 10–12; professional, 3–4; verbal, 3
Thoughts, substitution of, 102
Transpositions, 75–76
Trial and error, 39; in design, 34

Uncertainty: conditional, 15; contingent, 15; creation of, by type, 57–60; degrees of, 47; demonstration of, 10, 12–15; dimensions of, 57; and purpose, 60–61; and statistical analysis, 14; tests for, 12–14; uses of, 45–47; verbal, 89

Variance, statistical, for measuring uncertainty, 15
Vigotsky test, 26

White, Tom 102
Words, ambiguous, 87, 89; meaningful, 91

About the Author

RYLE L. MILLER, JR., was, prior to retirement, a registered engineer and editor for *Chemical Engineering* and *Chemical Week*, both published by McGraw-Hill. He has written or edited over 300 technical articles and five books.